10 Things
I Hate About
Christianity.

Working Through the
Frustrations of Faith.

by Jason T. Berggren

www.10thingsIhate.com

MEDIA

Making a mark

10 Things I Hate About Christianity: Working Through the Frustrations of Faith

2009 First Printing

Copyright © 2009 by Jason T. Berggren

ISBN: 9780981944302

Special discounts available for bulk purchases at http://10thingsihate.com.

Edited by Thomas Womack and Dawn Hurley
Cover and interior design by Kristen Lekberg,
with Creative Index Studio | www.thecistudio.com
Photo by Chrissy O'Neal

Published by X-Media LLC
Printed in the United States of America

This book is dedicated to those who continue to doubt, are curious about spiritual ideas, and are courageous enough to search them out. I consider you friends.

Contents

Why Hate?

I'm wrong. I usually am.

I'm not saying that to sound self-deprecating or to appear whimsical and charming in order to endear myself to you (though if it happens, I'm fine with that). I'm saying that because it's true. I know hate is wrong. I just don't know any other way to describe what I feel. It's to the point, direct, and yes, maybe even a little reckless and rude. But it's what I mean.

When I was growing up, my father—who's more civilized than I am—would strongly admonish me for using *hate* to describe my feelings about something or someone. He wanted me to understand how potent this word is. He was uncomfortable with its implied violence. He wanted me to use it cautiously.

I understand. But there are realities I must face.

Like Coca-Cola. I've loved Coke since I was a child. I would do fine never letting another beverage touch my lips for the rest of my life, not even water. I love the taste of the ice-cold liquid as it passes through my lips and cascades down my throat. I often say I'm a Coke addict as a joke, since it has such power over me. But the reality is that Coke isn't good for me in such large doses, and it causes me to gain weight. So, I *hate* the fact that I *love* Coke. It's a tension I have to learn to manage.

Unfortunately, this wrestling exists abundantly in the deeper, more important issues of my life as well.

My life is filled with personal conflict. This conflict has the power to crush my hopes and blur my dreams until they're merely memories of childhood fantasies, never again to be imagined, for fear of bringing even more tension, more confusion, more hate. Especially when the conflict is coupled with failure.

I used to dream of being a musician. When I was twelve, I worked through spring break and used my earnings to buy a cheap amp and guitar. I spent years teaching myself how to play. I would listen to tapes of my favorite bands, trying to copy the music and singing along. Eventually I began writing my own songs and even went on to be in a few bands.

In my early twenties, after investing time and money and delaying college, I finally realized I wasn't very good, so I quit. That is, not good enough to pay the bills. It was a heartbreaking reality to face. The experience was demoralizing and made me never want to pursue a dream again. They just weren't worth risking the heartache when they didn't come true. Is failure the end? Or is failure one of many steps to succeeding? Then there's the nagging, hovering cloud of *What ifs?* So, I continue to struggle.

When we're alone and being honest, most of us would admit

there's a deep personal war going on inside us. The smaller battles in this war break out in strange ways. They might drive us to eat a little too much dessert, spend a little too much on yet another pair of shoes, or have another drink. When left unchecked, conflict leads to confusion, regret, and guilt. And it grows. It may cause us to do things like insist on the last word in an argument and cause damage to a relationship we care about.

The truth remains: If we're to experience any peace, joy, or love as we learn to do life and relationships more successfully, our only option is to learn to fight our inner demons. We can't give up.

I hate all this tension, and I hate having to deal with it. It's a dilemma wrapped in a crisis stuck between a rock and a hard place.

But I've learned that this deep inner conflict can be a positive force. It can lead to a breakthrough and the opportunity for much-needed personal growth and renewal. We can train our minds to use our hate, and when we begin to sense it, we can create forward momentum: we sense the tension, wrestle with the issue, win the battle, learn a lesson, grow as an individual, and move ahead. This brings a new day with a new perspective and new opportunities.

× × × ×

There's nothing like watching the strength of the human spirit reaching forward in times of turmoil. This is why I put pen to paper. I'm just trying to chart a course through the murky waters of frustration and hate. I think I'm discovering a path through this fog, and I want to share it with you.

In this process, my faith has been key—which may surprise you, given this book's title. I am, in fact, a Christian, though I hesitate using the term because of the baggage that comes with it. Maybe it's better to say I'm trying to follow Jesus as closely as I can, like one of his twelve disciples. It's not easy. This may be why I like the disciples Thomas and Peter the most. Like them, I have many doubts and open my big mouth way too much.

This book is a log of my journey with faith, sometimes faltering, sometimes firm. It's a record of release and renewal, as I try to work toward contentment and wholeness.

So, I'm inviting you to hate with me—not the unguarded, irresponsible, and negative emotion my father often warned me about, but the inner sense of overwhelming dissatisfaction that can launch a progression toward personal growth. Identifying my feelings of hate has freed me to move forward. It has ignited a drive toward newness, discovering my potential, and the fulfillment that comes with that. It has also caused me to seek resolutions to bigger questions in my life: *Why are we all here? What's it all about? Is there more to it than this?*

These bigger questions are what led me to faith in Jesus. It was different than I expected, which I'll get into. But it was what I was looking for through my wrestling. I've found it to be the only way to achieve sanity.

Unfortunately, believing in him didn't fix everything. While I deeply admire, respect, and love Jesus, my faith in him has actually added to my inner struggles. And this is a real dilemma.

Faith can be a challenge and extremely inconvenient at times. Over and over, I've had to face certain aspects of my faith that don't seem to line up. I've been quite confused by what it means to seek

God's purpose for my life and to follow the teachings of Jesus. And while working through these questions, a truth became evident: *Wrong expectations lead to absolute frustration*. When we don't have all the facts, we usually end up disillusioned and angry—like when a couple thinks that having kids will make their relationship better. Then comes the rude awakening: more people equal more problems.

I'm constantly bumping up against this principle about wrong expectations because it pretty much applies everywhere. It has been especially true when it comes to my faith. If you remember only one thing from this book, make it that. It will help you in every arena of life—career, relationships, marriage, sex, having kids, faith, etc. I wish someone had told me about it a long time ago, so I'm telling you now.

Everyone has a story. This is mine—what I've actually hated about my faith at times, and how I'm working through it all. Maybe it can help you work out some of the issues in your own story.

Why Hate?

#1 Faith

Like many kids in America, I grew up playing baseball. At age seven, I skipped T-ball and went right to Pony League. It was extremely intimidating at first. This was real baseball, complete with the threat of being decapitated by a stray pitch. Kids were reckless. Everyone was trying to throw the ball as fast as possible, because speed equaled great pitching. Control was secondary.

After Pony League came Little League. Now pitching was something to really be afraid of. Kids were bigger, so speed increased dramatically. Unfortunately, the accuracy still wasn't there. Plus, the formula was still the same: speed equaled great pitching.

But for a nine-year-old, the challenge in moving up to Little League was striving to hit a homer, as every young boy wants to do.

The home run. It's what dreams are made of. When boys are staring into the clouds outside their classrooms, they're probably thinking about hitting home runs. When a mom has to scream for her son's attention, more than likely he's daydreaming about knocking one over the fence. When young kids have sleepovers and stay up way past bedtime, they're probably predicting how many long balls they'll hit next season.

I had home run dreams. I obsessed over them. And I was thrilled when I met our new neighbor Bill. He was an old-timer and told me about the glory of his Little League years. You know, "back in the day." I hung on his every word, because he said he could hit home runs at will. He even claimed to have hit home runs in every game. I fantasized about being him and living those moments. It seemed so unfair that he was so good.

But that was all about to change.

One day Bill told me his secret. I never felt so lucky in all my life, because his method wasn't magical at all. The next time I stepped up to the plate, I knew things would be different. This kid was going to give Hank Aaron a run for his money. As Bill explained it, all I had to do was *keep my eye on the ball*. Simply watch it leave the pitcher's hand until it hits the bat, and BAM! A home run. "Don't try to kill it," he added. "Just make contact." After that, I never took another swing without my eyes locked on the ball. But I never hit a home run. *Never.*

I began to resent my neighbor. His advice didn't yield a mantle full of home run balls, the admiration of teammates, fear from opponents, or attention from girls. All I wanted was the thrill of hearing the crack of the bat as the ball sailed away from me, the victory lap around the diamond, the applause of the crowd, and the home movie immortalizing the moment. I wanted what so many other kids seemed to get. But it just never happened for me. I couldn't accept that I wasn't good enough or that I was doing something wrong. It was *his* fault. I felt as if Bill had lied, and so I surmised that all his stories were probably lies too.

As my temper took hold, I did what kids did to other neighbors they didn't like. I lit a flaming bag of dog poo on his welcome mat and rang the doorbell so he would be forced to answer the door and stamp it out. Hot dog poo everywhere! *[Not really. He was too close to my home.]* But it was hard to resist the urge to take vengeance on him. I wanted a guarantee. I wanted to know how to control the outcome, but I couldn't. I'd been given a false sense of hope, and the results, or lack thereof, crushed me. After that season, I never played baseball again.

Not much has changed since Little League. I'm pretty good at most things I put my mind to, but not really amazing at anything. I'm also not very lucky. I've never been in the right place at the right time. I can't help you get a crazy deal on a set of tires, and I've never won an all-expenses-paid cruise to Cozumel. I find myself just having to work hard at every little thing in life.

And a familiar feeling (much like my failed home run dreams) eventually brought my faith in Jesus to a breaking point. I was reaching for purpose and meaning, but I found new questions and new problems. I started feeling as if I wasn't good enough for the "Jesus team," or maybe I was doing something wrong, and I wanted to quit. I often wondered if there was a way to find an angel with a sense of humor so he could help me place a flaming bag of poo in front of heaven's pearly gates for St. Peter to answer and stamp out. (I suppose I have passive aggressive tendencies in my spirituality too.)

Something wasn't quite right with my faith; it wasn't working out that great for me. I started to wonder: what's the point of having faith if it isn't even helping?

The Small Print

There's always fine print, isn't there? A friend offering a free lunch comes with a catch like, "By the way, do you mind feeding my pet iguana his live bugs this weekend while I'm away? And while you're there feeding Leonard, could you pick up my mail too?" Don't you hate that?

I thought faith would dispel all the unknown variables and problems in my life. It seemed reasonable to think that if I took Jesus seriously, God would answer all my questions and take away all my problems. I thought it was a good deal. But it seemed to take a wrong turn, because he didn't come through. Didn't he understand I didn't want to live with so much confusion? I was so mad at him, and I wanted to take back the commitment I made. (To be fair, I don't think it was totally his fault, but I still get mad over it.)

One thing I hate about my faith is the fantasy element. There's Santa Claus, the Easter Bunny, the Tooth Fairy, God, and Jesus. We teach kids they're *all* real, but they're not *all* real. Eventually our kids will be okay with Santa, the Easter Bunny, and the Tooth Fairy being cute little white lies, while accepting Jesus and God as completely legit—right? Now I know the intentions are good, but I wonder if it's unfair. Could this also set us up for almost certain disillusionment as we grow up and inevitably question the existence of God and consequently the meaning of our own existence? I've had many a conversation with people trying to figure out how to work through this, and it's not easy. Many times, they hit a wall, and I totally understand.

In any other context, believing this "lie" would be clinical. For instance, imagine you and I run into each other somewhere and I ask if you would like to meet my friend Jane. You respond, "Sure!" With hand extended, you reach around me to find no one. But I insist. I'm adamant about her being right here with us. I even tell you how much Jane loves you and wants to help you in your life. Undoubtedly, you would give me a casual smile as you contemplated making a secret phone call. The whole episode could end with me being escorted off the scene in a white jacket with lots of extra straps and shiny belt buckles, remarking how much better this thing would look in black leather. You would call me crazy, and you would be right.

Do I expect people to think it's any less delusional because my friend's name is Jesus? I admit it. The *whole having a relationship with someone who isn't physically there, and talking to him on a regular basis (praying)* is weird, to say the least, and eccentric, at best. If only God and Jesus would appear every so often around town to buy sneakers at the mall to prove to everyone they're real, it would make all this a little easier. But they don't, and it makes me mad. *I'll be expecting my jacket anytime now.*

Once I can get past the fantasy element, I have to deal with feeling stupid. I hate feeling stupid. Who doesn't? It seems like I always have to face the fact that having faith isn't really an intellectual exercise. There really are no facts and figures to prove (or disprove) the existence of God or what I believe, and that makes me feel dumb.

If I were talking to someone who considered himself somewhat intellectual and fairly intelligent and rational (as most people do), and he was explaining to me how he came to a certain large-scale, life-altering decision, I wouldn't be surprised to hear him say it involved reading some academic research, pondering certain intellectual principles, and weighing lots of empirical evidence. Maybe he would even pull out some graphs and pie charts. And his decision would make total sense to me. But when I describe my own life-altering decision, it's a little different.

I always end up in pretty much the same place. "Yes, I believe in Jesus. I can't really explain it. It's a decision I made based on a feeling. And I trust in the sincerity of that feeling." Unavoidably, there's a sense of embarrassment. And I *hate* that. It's not that I'm ashamed of what I believe or who I believe in. I know it to be true. It's just an awkward situation by default. Not to mention the many people who already think having faith is simply superstitious, primitive, and irrational.

I know I would sound more introspective, informed, and perceptive by pointing out flaws or being more skeptical and *not* believing. But I can't, because I *do* believe. There are, in fact, volumes of reference materials that try to deal with faith in the academic arena and do a fine job of intellectualizing a faith decision. In the end, however, all these scholars and philosophers arrive at much the same place as me: faith is essentially a decision based on a feeling. There's just no way around it. But I hate having to push through that every single time I talk about what I believe.

Another thing I especially hate is the seemingly broken promise.

As I've indicated, I like guarantees and predictability. I want to be able to forecast and control the outcomes in my life. Faith was supposed to bring clarity in my confusion, answering all my questions and helping me make total sense of life. This would give me the ability and confidence to make the best decisions in all situations, thereby ensuring that only good and beneficial things happen in my life—total peace all the time. Sometimes it gave me peace, but mostly it didn't, and I felt like God was letting me down.

My confusion multiplied with the number of forks in the road. Should I buy a car or lease it? What should I major in? When should I get married? When should we have kids? Can I even afford a kid? Is this the right house to buy? We all have our own lists of unpredictable situations, and mine gets longer the older I get, as life grows more complicated. I find living with so many unknowns to be quite unsettling.

The fact is, I knew absolutely nothing about faith. In an effort to fire me up in my commitment and keep me devoted to Jesus, some Christians early on seemed to inadvertently "sell me" on this cure-all idea of faith, like some kind of acne medicine that could clear everything up and help me get a really hot girlfriend. Christian television and radio reinforced it, telling me things like "name it and claim it!" With enough faith, I'd be able to create and control the outcomes in my life and get whatever I wanted. Like Luke Skywalker using "the force," I could move objects around in my life and make people do what I wanted with my Jedi mind-tricks. And if my faith wasn't doing those things for me, I just didn't have enough of it.

I liked the idea, but it didn't work. This obviously meant

something wasn't right, and I felt like I was it. I was doing something wrong; I wasn't good enough.

Where were the guarantees? Where was the security? The good deal turned raw, and I wanted my money back.

All these issues brought a dose of reality I wasn't prepared for. I mean, who wants to trust his whole life to someone nobody can see? Who wants to tell others about this very nebulous personal decision? And who wants to keep up the commitment when things don't exactly work out like we think they should, making it all look pointless?

That's the fine print no one ever told me about. It's been twenty years, and sometimes I still feel like I'm about to come apart. These things still go with the territory.

I still get mad sometimes. But as I pushed through these issues and worked them out, I began to discover the true value of my faith. I would have robbed myself had I shut down and let my hate and frustration defeat my faith and newfound purpose.

I have to be up-front. I owe a lot of this to an old friend of mine who caused me to think through this stuff. It's an old conversation, but it's why I have an enduring faith today. That conversation illustrates the process of my faith.

The Other Jason

It's always strange when you meet someone with the same name as you. It's even weirder when you're alike. I met Jason during my high school years, and he became a good friend. He didn't go to my school, but one of his best friends was in most of my classes, so we hung out periodically. Eventually, I caught up with Jason at community college, and that's when we became better friends.

We had a similar schedule on Tuesdays and Thursdays. We would hang out in the cafeteria between classes, usually grabbing breakfast or lunch if it looked edible enough. He always wanted to play chess, but I despised the game. It took too much thought. I'm more of a checkers kind of guy. I was at community college, after all. So, we talked instead. We were young guys, so we talked movies, music, and girls. Eventually we started talking about spiritual stuff because we were both curious.

I wasn't as smart as he was, but I communicated the best I could. I started telling him things I'd been wondering about and how I'd come to believe in the life and teachings of Jesus. This subject became the basis of our ongoing dialogue, as he challenged premise after premise that I presented. Inside, I hated his apprehensions, but I began to appreciate them as he stated his questions with respect. He seemed to be tracking with me and gauging his spiritual search along the way. Our dialogue went on for nearly a year.

He first challenged me to explain why I would believe in someone or something I couldn't see. I acknowledged it was a strange practice. I thought it through a little more, and the next time I saw him, I told him I just couldn't ignore something going on within me (and it had nothing to do with the cafeteria food). I started to sense a void deep inside. In no particular order, I was overwhelmed by the randomness and despair in life, I was struggling with a sense of purpose for my future, and I was increasingly convinced there was a spiritual element to our existence. That was the framework for my void.

Just acknowledging these realities brought an initial sense of relief, though it soon yielded a greater sense of responsibility.

I told Jason I was noticing and thinking about things I never had before, and I couldn't stop. Clearly there was more to us than flesh, blood, and bones. I mentioned how some of our classes might actually be backing this up. In Chemistry, my professor tried to rationalize the mystery of why an atom remains intact and the universe doesn't fly apart. She taught us about "cosmic glue," "dark matter," and "X." To me, this fit what I was discovering spiritually. But to explain the unknown, there had to be more than overly generous, sweeping, generic, catchall descriptions. I told Jason I thought there was a spiritual element to life that these deficient descriptions were touching on. Specifically, hidden deep down inside him, somewhere between his heart, soul, and mind, I was convinced there was a spiritual being, something all the science in the world could never explain. It's in all of us. It explains who we really are, and it has little to do with blood or guts or cosmic glue.

Besides, there's so much about our existence that can't be explained. So believing in something I couldn't see wasn't a big issue for me, since we all do it to some degree. It was more a matter of what to do with that knowledge. Would I ignore it? Or try to make sense of it? Was there a reason for, and behind, all this mystery?

Jason could see how I got to that point. It made some sense to him, as he was having similar thoughts. But he still wasn't sure if he was willing to have faith in something he couldn't see or prove.

I said I understood. I also reinforced the idea that we all believe in someone or something. We all rely on a set of beliefs or core values, not necessarily religious in nature, that guide us at unsure times. Perhaps people seek the advice of good friends, parents or grandparents, take a class, or read a book. The resulting beliefs and values they develop aren't visible, but people trust in them. So, I argued, we all look at the situations we're facing, consider what we believe, and then leap. This functions much like faith. For the most part, we're all trusting in things we can't see—a type of faith, to some degree. I was simply bringing it to the next level and choosing to be influenced and mentored by Jesus.

He saw my point. We finished our waffles and went off to our classes.

The next time I saw Jason, he asked why I would trust in God even when things weren't exactly going great. He'd often observed bad things happening to people of faith, and it made him wonder: what's the point? There had to be some immediate benefit to faith, if it was worth anything at all. Or maybe God wasn't as involved in our lives as people liked to think: either he didn't care all that much, or wasn't that powerful.

"Fair question," I admitted. This was his version of the "broken promise" and "guarantee" thing that had angered me.

I came back the next time, ordered my pizza and tater-tots, filled my cup with Coke, and told him my additional thoughts on the subject. I had to believe that regardless of how things were going, there still had to be a rhyme or reason greater than myself.

Part of this was just out of necessity. I talked about my growing sense of needing certain absolutes with regard to truth. There was a part of me that didn't want to be the sole authority in my life anymore, the sole decider of what was right and wrong. With just me, I could remodel my right and wrong at any time simply to make them more convenient, and that was too chaotic and dangerous. It made everything too relative and fluid. It meant that ultimately I couldn't find the meaning in life I desperately wanted out of all these spiritual musings because there was nothing certain to build on.

I told Jason I was convinced there had to be a measure that was true, regardless of outcomes. Bad stuff happening or things not working out right did not mean there was no God. That stuff was another issue altogether (which I'd have to deal with later).

Jason remarked that perhaps my relationship to God was based less on what I was getting out of the situation and more on *who* was going with me through life as I experienced it.

"Exactly!" I answered.

He said he'd never thought of it like that before—as a relationship. He compared it to hopefully being married and having kids in the future. His wife wouldn't fix all his problems and make life perfect, but sharing his life with someone he loved deeply, and who loved him, would definitely make life better.

There was more I needed to say. I admitted I still sensed frustration, since I wanted life to be a lot easier and safer and without so many variables, so much unpredictability. But I had to be fair to God. Faith had, in fact, brought me more clarity and confidence— just not to the level I wanted or expected. Yet, without a doubt, I was better off now than when I functioned without faith.

I ended with this: *My faith actually gives me the ability to navigate life in the midst of the unknown.*

He said that was somewhat similar to what he was saying, and I agreed. The bottom line was: things may not be perfect or perfectly easy, but my life was better with faith.

We cleaned our trays and went on with our days.

Jason later admitted he often viewed faith as a crutch. I'd heard this many times and found it insulting, but I didn't know how to respond. Was there no way faith could find a home in the heart of the truly strong-minded, independent, freethinking person?

I came back the next Thursday and confessed I agreed with Jason. I even took it one step further. For me, faith was more like a wheelchair or one of those motorized things old people drive around in the grocery store. I was beginning to gain a little life experience, and to realize that when I'm down-and-out, beaten up emotionally, or at my wits' end, faith is the only reason I can press on.

I also submitted the idea that those who live by their sincere faith are in fact quite strong and resolute, maybe even the strongest of individuals. Faith can propel people forward against all odds and carry them through the storms of failure and discouragement. They may act against practical thinking and pragmatic theories, but they don't care. They have a drive in them that's amazing, like Rocky Balboa in the boxing ring. And no matter what they're facing, they see each situation as an opportunity.

I said that in the hearts of the willing, faith could lead to achievements of epic proportions. Because of my own faith, I knew I was learning to pick myself up, dust myself off, and keep going in tough times. "Yes," I told him, "I lean on my faith, because I'm weaker on my own."

The next time I saw Jason, he asked me something I didn't want to answer, and it was big. This was really the last major theme we discussed. (Everything afterward was mostly a rehash of ideas we'd already covered.) Jason asked why I found the Christian faith and philosophy more interesting than any other. Why did I think it was true?

That was a hard one. Not that I didn't know, but I knew my answer would be kind of polarizing.

When we got together again, I told him I wasn't interested in religion, specifically. What was compelling to me was the spirituality Jesus spoke of and the context for it he created. What Jesus said was relational, making it different from the systems our World Religions class revealed, which were legalistic (working our way into heaven) or fatalistic (you're doomed no matter what you do in life). I understood that Jesus wanted to spend eternity with me, and even go with me through this life, just because he loves me. There's nothing I have to do to earn his love, and I can do nothing to drive it away. All I had to do was sincerely believe.

This gave me a sense of value. My parents had separated when I was very young, and growing up I never felt particularly valuable or valued; I pretty much felt like an inconvenience, like something disposable. That loomed over me. But what Jesus said finally washed all that away. He gave me a blank page, a new beginning, a reason to set some goals and even dream a little—because my life mattered. My future did too.

It also challenged me to grow, to always be willing to stretch myself. I already didn't like some things I was turning into. I was developing some addictive habits, had a tendency to get angry, and was typically negative and pessimistic. Reading the words of Jesus, I decided he wanted me to never be too impressed with myself. He challenged me somehow to question the status quo, reach beyond my limitations, and test my potential.

Just think, I told Jason, about those first twelve followers of Jesus. They were a rag-tag team of misfits. Most were rough and working class. Some were even hated for their professions. They were just average people, not particularly gifted or successful. No fame, power, position, or influence to speak of.

At first, this discouraged Jason's view of the Christian faith, as if those men weren't qualified to represent God. He even wondered why Jesus would pick them.

But look at the flip side, I told him. God didn't want perfect people, just *willing* people. And when Jesus said, "Follow me," they did. And because of those devoted misfits, we're still talking about Jesus two thousand years later. He continues to be the most influential person in history because of that handful of failures and undesirables that found value and purpose and were willing to challenge the possibilities, even under the threat of death, in those early days of the Christian faith. And that's what Jesus wanted me to do—to keep going, to keep growing, to keep reaching forward.

I also mentioned how Jesus inspired me. Sometimes life just plain sucks; we can't control it, and there's no way to change our surroundings. The only thing that helps is a little comfort as we wade through all the garbage. Jesus gave me hope. He said his spirit would be inside my heart during those times to comfort me. There was something to look forward to, the promise of a better day. This helped me endure whatever situation I was facing. To me, that's really what hope is.

I was convinced that a life without hope was no life at all. Life was filled with so many personal failures and overall difficulties.

Life was hard much more than it was easy. And when people lose hope (which is easy to do)—nothing to live for or look forward to— something dies inside.

I ended by saying that I thought we all wanted something more in our lives than to just exist. My faith gave me this—a sense of value, a reason to dream, a reason to grow and become a better person, and hope to inspire me.

The Deciding Factor

It was amazing. The next time I saw Jason, he said something I never expected. After our months and months of talking, he said he was totally convinced that what I'd discovered was true. I couldn't believe it! But he also said he wasn't ready to make the change and decide just yet. He had to think it through a little more to be fully convinced. I didn't really understand that, but I gave him some space.

That's where we pretty much left things. From then on, I decided to let him initiate any spiritual conversations.

It became awkward when I saw him. It was as if he was avoiding deeper conversation. We mainly talked about what was going on with him, and it wasn't pretty. To get through it, I thought he needed faith more than anything. I wanted him to experience some of the peace, contentment, purpose, and clarity I'd begun to have. But I didn't press it. I wanted to, but he was becoming distant, so I wanted to give him some room. I knew he had to make the connection himself. We'd spent a year building our friendship, and I didn't want to ruin it by being overly enthusiastic and appear like I had some agenda (though in a way I did, but for a good reason).

Jason always had a hard time at home. His dad was never around. As a result, his mom looked to him for everything. She turned her relationship with him into some warped kind of husband-friend-son combination. He had to do everything around the house, help with the bills, and listen to all her woes and somehow try to fix them. It had been like this for a long time, and it got to be too much. He had to get out.

That's about the time our conversations became shallow. He moved in with a friend who had an apartment with his girl-friend. Jason had to sleep on their couch, but I think it was an improvement.

Things were better for a while, but then got worse. Jason's mom wouldn't leave him alone. She called him and showed up at his job. She told him how much he let her down, what a jerk and failure he was, and how worthless he was to leave her just like his dad had.

Jason finally decided to make another change.

I hadn't seen him at school for a couple weeks. This wasn't completely unusual, since we both had jobs, papers, and projects to balance. Plus, since Jason wasn't living at home, it was hard to phone him. (Not everyone had cell phones back then; they were the size of a brick and really expensive.) Finally, I asked another friend if he'd seen him. He hadn't, but he knew where he was. He told me the story someone else told him.

One day Jason quit his job, withdrew from school, closed his bank account, and left a note to explain everything for his room-mates and the rest of us. When the roommates came back late that night, they found the note on the coffee table. It was right in front of Jason's couch, where his dead body was lying. He'd purchased a gun with his last dollars and killed himself.

I was devastated.

There Jason and I were again, like back in high school, at a social function together. Except that this was his funeral. Jason's mom even read his suicide letter aloud. She was emotional and weeping and seemed strangely ambivalent to the parts in it related to her. It was uncomfortable, and I just wanted to leave. It was one of the saddest moments of my life. It was so empty and hopeless, and I felt partly responsible in some way. If only Jason and I could have had one more talk.

I know it's a heavy story. Jason had a big effect on me, and his story is part of my story. He challenged what I believed and caused me to really examine it. And he helped me learn one last lesson in his final act: everyone makes a decision about God. Even the atheist or agnostic decides something. Even no decision is a decision.

I just wish my friend had made the decision I wanted him to make.

When Jason and I talked, I never wanted to be overly enthusiastic, press too hard, and turn him off. I wondered, how far is too far? When do conversations on faith become pushy and self-defeating rather than a healthy and productive discourse on important spiritual issues that have eternal consequences? It's a balance I still struggle with today when talking to friends, family, or people I meet or work with. Most of the time I choose to opt out of those conversations, so I can seem more normal. That bothers me, because no one's guaranteed another day. You never know about tomorrow.

As I've come to understand the value of my faith, it has become clear that faith is the reason good times are better and it makes hard times livable. I think that's essentially the promise God does make to humanity as we place our faith in him—he's still with us regardless of how we feel. It's a compelling promise, and I trust in it.

Don't get me wrong, I still doubt from time to time. But I think it's normal to doubt. In fact, I don't even view it as the opposite of faith. Some think it is, but that's unfair. In the same way that caution isn't always the opposite of risk, or fear isn't the opposite of courage, doubt is not the opposite of faith. They can be present at the same time. There's always a measure of caution when balancing a risky decision. There's also a sense of fear to sober us as we advance in a courageous endeavor. And there's always a sense of doubt that tests and purifies my faith as I step forward with it. I just believe what Jesus said is true.

To me, faith is the unknown revealed and explained. Having faith may seem irrational to you—and I assure you, it is. With faith it's strangely possible to acknowledge the unexplained, face it, embrace it, and move forward. It's not a mindless devotion to antiquated ideas or benevolent ideals, but a calculated conclusion in the light of present reality: there's more unknown than known. It's a coming to terms with the mystery of life. It's the strength to keep a conviction when surrounded by questions. It's discovering twenty variables and one truth, then holding to that truth regardless of the present ambiguities. It can go against better judgment and modern thought, while being the wiser approach.

My faith is still a mystery in many ways, which drives me insane, but I also know it's the one thing that's true.

Maybe that's my home run.

#2 Prayer

I once had an office job, which took some adjusting to. I'm a hands-on type of person, and I like going different places and doing different things. Sitting at a desk was much more controlled and confined than I was used to. I gained twenty pounds from the change of pace.

One day I was sitting at my desk trying to get in contact with the person in the next office. His door was closed, so I wasn't sure if he was in a meeting or something. My need wasn't immediate, so I sent him an email. No reply. As time went on the issue became more pressing, so I sent him an IM over the computer. No response. Next, I called him on the office phone. I got his voicemail. I called him on his cell phone. More voicemail. I tried beeping him on the two-way radio feature our phones had. Nothing.

Finally, I got up and knocked on the door. He told me to come in. We discussed the matter to my satisfaction, and I went back to my office.

Thanks to today's amazing technology, I had at my disposal a variety of ways to communicate with my coworker. But though I wasn't more than fifteen feet away from him, we weren't any more connected relationally than before all these advances were available. In fact, we were more distant. They made our interaction less personal and, therefore, less effective. Even with all the new possibilities, the old-school, face-to-face talking worked best.

There are no such technological advances to scroll through when I'm trying to connect with God. In fact, there's only one way—simply talking to him, or *praying*, as we say. No double and triple function buttons to fumble through with my fat fingers as I try to fire off a quick message.

Still, most of the time I feel like it doesn't work, and I feel distant from God. Quite often, it turns out to be even less personal than any other communicating I do. I don't feel any more connected with him afterward. And I hate that.

I hate feeling like it doesn't work. I hate feeling distant. I hate feeling disconnected. I feel like it's pointless. I often wonder if there's something I could do differently. Or is it a futile undertaking?

Can You Hear Me Now?

Everybody knows long distance relationships (LDRs) usually don't work. The love interest you had in the Niagara Falls area probably isn't the person you married and had kids with. The odds are stacked against it. I've met a few couples that started out as LDRs and managed to finish well together, but it's rare.

I find trying to build closeness with God through prayer is ten times worse than any other LDR. It's an LDR that spans not only the world, not just the universe, but even different dimensions. I mean, who exactly am I talking to? Where is he? *Ground control to Major God! Do you hear me? I sure don't hear you.*

Now I've met people who claim they "hear from God" all the time. And I've tried to get away from them quickly. Those words always seem to be the precursor to an individual's evolution into a serial killer. Those words are just foreign to me.

When I pray, my words seem to evaporate and hit the ceiling. I pour out my heart in hopes of feeling a touch or getting some interaction with God, but it seems he doesn't answer. And I hate being left hanging and all alone. I never hear his comforting voice. God's door is closed, and I just want some face-to-face time. It's kind of a tease—a cosmic one. It's not what I expected when it comes to talking to God.

I think most people probably feel this distance at some point, yet they continue praying. Even the hard-line atheist calls on God before rear-ending the car in front of him at full speed: "Oh God, *help!*" It's funny—everyone prays. I think everyone feels like it's a good habit with some therapeutic benefit. But still we wonder: does it work, or is it pointless?

Dear Dad

If you've seen the movie *A Christmas Story,* you know it's an endearing look at the holiday season set around 1940, with a little more realism than usual. It's funny, because it's true.

A young boy, Ralphie, wants a BB gun for Christmas. But everyone—the department store Santa, his parents, his teacher—tells him that's a bad idea because he'll shoot his eye out. He only begs and pleads even more.

On Christmas morning, after all the gifts are opened, Ralphie sits there disappointed. Then his parents bring out one more gift for him. After ripping off the wrapping—yes, it's a Red Ryder BB gun—he immediately runs outside to try it.

And promptly shoots his eye out.

Just kidding. Actually, a ricochet hits him just below the eye and when he flinches, his glasses come off, which he then steps on and breaks. Now he realizes the truth of what his parents were telling him. They were just trying to protect him. His parents knew better, but Ralphie couldn't accept that. So, he tells his mom an icicle fell off the edge of the roof and hit him in the eye, breaking his glasses.

Most of the time what I hate about prayer is that I tend to be a lot like Ralphie. My perspective is limited.

In relating to God, I think of him mostly as a parent, a father specifically. That's probably natural for most people, but it can be problematic. Maybe your dad left when you were young. Maybe he died. Or maybe your dad was there, but just never that involved in your life. He was too busy to take you to soccer practice or even go to the games. Maybe he gave you a lot of rules without a relationship, which probably made you rebel rather than respect him. More importantly, maybe he didn't teach you how to be smart with money, build a great career, or pick a good spouse.

Everybody has family issues. I don't want to blame all my hang-ups on that. But here's a truth I've learned: how I relate to my father deeply affects how I relate to God. Working through this has been the first step in helping me as I approach God in prayer. But it's still hard.

My dad was a good man. But he also told me no a lot. And he often made promises that never came to be. I'm sure his shortcomings had a lot to do with his own dad being an alcoholic or even his growing up in a socialist society in Sweden (that's another subject).

By default I assume that God, like my dad, is telling me no when praying doesn't turn out like I want. I realize this isn't necessarily true, but it's the lens I see through when praying.

I suppose it could be worse. I knew a kid named T. J. in my neighborhood who at age ten was already was on his fifth stepfather. I can't imagine how difficult relating to God might be for his sister and him.

And here's something else to consider on this father-image idea, if you believe that God has an enemy, the devil. To win against you, that enemy doesn't necessarily have to get you to become an atheist or a Satanist or something crazy like that. He simply has to devalue the role of fathers in our lives and our culture. Then people will naturally gravitate away from the concept of God as they relate to him in the same way they do to their own bad, distant, or absentee fathers.

Think about television shows. If there's a dad, he's most likely a bumbling idiot who can't get anything right. Or he's never around and working too much. Or he's cheating or leaving his family. There's plainly a cultural undercurrent that treats moms as absolutely necessary in the lives of children (which they are) and dads as secondary and unnecessary. It's no wonder we all complain about the shortage of strong fathers or that men don't act like men. As the children of these fathers become adults, they may never see a need for God or even believe in him. That's a tragedy. As a father of three, I try to never let myself forget that my children will base their views of God on how they see me. That's quite a responsibility.

So, in prayer, as best as I can, I work hard against my natural tendency to see God through a bad lens. I visualize him as the perfect dad—present, supportive, encouraging, and wise. He's strong and sensitive at the same time. He's faithful and involved. He always has time. And he always knows best. I value him, and he values me. This may sound silly, but it really has started to work. It's the first step in giving me a better perspective on prayer.

God@allsignspointtoyes.hvn

I've also tried to break down how I pray and what I pray for.

First, I pray for specific answers.

That can be scary. When I was growing up, my friend had a Magic 8-Ball. You asked it a yes-or-no question, shook it, then turned it over and read the answer it mysteriously granted. When we had sleepovers, we would sit on his bedroom floor all night asking it questions to find out what to expect in our futures. My friends always seemed to get awesome answers. They were destined to be rich, famous, and powerful. But the Magic 8-Ball would tell me things like: "My sources say no." "Outlook not so good." "Don't count on it." I never received the life-affirming, much-coveted, golden answer: "All signs point to yes!"

I've had a habit of turning God into an oracle of luck. He's the Magic 8-Ball. I shake him by throwing out my questions and expecting the answers to float to the top. I just wish he would answer more often, "All signs point to yes." Actually, I'd even take "My reply is no." Either answer would bring a measure of relief and closure.

I pray for answers in everything. It's usually the first thing I do when I pray, and my intentions are good. But when I don't get a yes or no for the particular situation I'm facing, I get more discouraged. Then not only do I have this sense of insecurity about the situation, as well as disappointment over my prayers not working, but now I'm mad. This makes it even more difficult to decide what to do.

Facing that kind of hold-up, I decided early on I wasn't going to wait for God. I began creating a formula to lean on when I didn't get specific answers from God. It went something like this: If a "door opens" (or something works out), *it's meant to be*; if a "door closes" (something doesn't work out), it's *not meant to be*. So if something is going well and I feel good about it, keep it up; it's an implied yes from God. If something gets hard and I'm frustrated, quit; it's an understood no.

If I couldn't make God into a Magic 8-Ball, I'd turn him into a game of rock-paper-scissors.

That's when things really started to go wrong.

Though it took quite some time to get through my thick skull, I eventually figured out that this formula didn't work. In the things I've been part of that have failed or succeeded, one thing's clear: there are more closed doors than open ones. And the open doors can often be diversions from what's best.

You probably know this if you've ever been part of starting something from scratch. Maybe a do-it-yourself project at home. Or launching a business. Or you're after some training or a degree. I'm guessing you met more closed doors than open ones. It was probably just 80 to 90 percent hard labor and plowing through it all to make it work. That's why they call these things "labors of love." And I bet some of the options and opportunities that seemed good turned out to be setbacks. They really were *too good to be true*.

If you ever have the opportunity to sit down and have breakfast with someone who's really succeeded at something, don't pass it up. I've done this a few times, and it has been invaluable. In each story, I've found common themes.

First, they're not sure why their ventures succeeded while other people's failed. There wasn't something different or secret they did. They simply had a decent idea, were passionate about their vision, worked hard, and remained diligent. And at a certain point, usually when they were ready to give up (often about two years in), something began to catch on. They began getting traction and building momentum.

Another common thread I noticed in these stories is that the things worth doing were usually hidden behind closed doors that needed to be kicked in. They had to fight to keep their ideas alive if they really believed in them. Or, as I once heard it put, "There's no such thing as luck or fate, only that which we create."

I'm not saying all wide-open doors should be avoided and all closed doors battered down. I'm just saying it's dangerous to interpret yes or no answers from God based on the ease of moving forward. Doing that will make you even more angry with God, because the results of that strategy are inconsistent.

Maybe you're thinking, "Wait a minute. I once heard how God opens doors that no man can close, and he closes doors no man can open. Isn't that in the Bible somewhere?" Exactly! But I've noticed that when God opens and closes doors, it often defies the natural course of events we would expect. It's obviously his doing and not some concocted mystical formula of ours. Something bigger than us intervened. What happened is strange. It doesn't add up. And there's no mistaking God did it.

A while back, we moved to a less expensive place to reduce our cost of living and to create some freedom in my schedule so I could work on my first book (this one). But after a year, I had little to show for it. My book was still pretty much a figment of my imagination. I was working a lot and commuting about two to three hours a day. And weekends were burned up on home projects and time with the kids. No one took me seriously when I talked about my book, especially my friends. I felt like some longhaired kid wearing a tie-dyed T-shirt and sandals, driving around the country in my Volkswagen bus, smoking-out and talking about how to change the world.

I needed to change something.

Then I noticed how most everyone I met in our community in the North Metro Atlanta area was in the technology industry, and they all had honey-do lists of things they couldn't do, or couldn't get to because of their busy lives. So, I let go of a steady income by quitting my job with a friend doing remodeling work in the city, and I advertised myself for handyman work. I incorporated, made a cool logo, and printed up signs and cards—I was targeting professionals, so I needed to look professional. Every weekend I put out signs and handed out cards in parking lots.

My approach was risky. I refused to do estimates, which may sound strange. But the types of jobs I was targeting were random (hang a fan, fix a leaky pipe, replace some rotten wood). Often they were only a few hours long. So, I marketed a flat rate (which was more than double what my hourly rate had been in remodeling). I told clients I would tackle these assorted small jobs on their lists and simply bill for my time. As odd as all that sounded (to my wife and me as well as to our friends), this new approach worked.

It was miraculous. I would be booked solid for two weeks, then right when I started running out of work, calls would come in and fill my schedule back up. Knowing I had a family to support, this got unnerving at times, but there's no doubt something mysterious was going on.

At one point, I had no work the next day. That night my wife and I were on our way to meet up with a group of friends for dinner. The babysitter was early, so we left the house early. My wife said we needed dish sponges, so we stopped by the grocery store we like. For some reason they stopped carrying the kind of sponges she likes, so we had to go to another grocery store— the one we hate to go to (I know this sounds trivial, but if you're married, you know about these quirks). While we were getting out of our car, a guy pulled up nearby. He was just popping in to get one thing, some Parmesan cheese for his family of seven. Seeing my sign on the car, he asked for a card.

For the last six months, this guy has kept me busy two to three days a week. All because my wife had to have a specific dish sponge. It's obvious God is working in our lives, because this kind of thing isn't natural.

Some people might view this as luck. To us it was clearly God answering our prayers. He was making my handyman idea work so we could pay our bills, and with the added flexibility in my schedule, I could work on my book.

This is just one example. But the whole course of events, as minor as they were, seemed clearly orchestrated. When God opens or closes a door in that way, it's obviously him. At least that's how I see it.

Maybe it's happened with you. You submit an offer on a house. You're prequalified for the loan, you've offered more than the asking price with no contingencies, and there are no other offers on the table. Everything couldn't be more right. But for some reason, it doesn't happen. No explanation. Nothing. It doesn't make a bit of sense. It defies the natural and logical course of events. You don't get the house. Then three weeks later the company transfers you, and it all makes sense.

Or maybe it's a position you're not qualified for, but you submit your résumé anyway. To your surprise, you get the job over a half-dozen more qualified applicants. It defies the natural and conventional wisdom—you can't explain it. It's clearly God. It may not always be the answer we want, but there's obviously something answered through the course of events that really stands out.

Subject: Just Do It (Or Something)

Still, there's the frustration of figuring out what to do when I get no specific answer from God, and I still have to press on.

I'm like that with my kids too. I don't answer all their questions. I often ask them what they think, and then let them take action (within reasonable and safe limits). And as they grow and mature, I give them even bigger challenges.

I want them to not depend on me for every little thing. Sure, Dad will always be there for them, but they also need to make their own decisions in life. They need to learn to succeed. And they need to know how to fail. That will ultimately help them best.

It's not that I don't love them or don't want to give them answers. I love the fact that they need me. But I also want them to figure things out for themselves based on what I've already taught them. I don't want them to stay immature forever and eventually become irresponsible. I don't want them still living at home well into their thirties. I'll want a break by then, if I'm not dead already.

I see God as this type of loving father. Sometimes what I view as an unanswered prayer may just be God wanting to see what his kid will do with what he has learned. As we pray about a decision or a direction, I think he wants us to take in as much information as possible, reflect on past experiences, and make a move.

It's not that he's uninvolved or distant. I just think he gets a thrill when we exercise our free wills and use our gifts and abilities. He wants to see what we'll do with what he has given us. Any other approach wouldn't mature us. It would undermine our responsibility in this life. Faithfulness, hard work, and strategy would take a backseat.

I was once told that God very often does supernatural things through very natural means. I've branded that on my heart. It reminds me that I'm responsible for making an effort, as much as I'm able. Maybe not getting an answer isn't all that bad.

Sitting around and waiting for answers sounds spiritual, but I can't hide my lack of courage and insecurities behind that, trying to dodge the difficulties that usually come with taking action. As annoying as it is, adversity yields character. I feel like my generation is losing the treasure of old-timers who learned the ancient lessons: *Life's hard, and there are no shortcuts.* Anything really worth doing will take effort, and lots of it.

I'm also under the impression that God can't do much with our inaction. He wants us to do *something*. God typically doesn't create something from nothing (except when he first made the universe). He usually makes something from something. Like when Jesus turned water into wine.

Our goals are the start of that. They give us targets and keep us from sitting around and waiting. And they give him a heads-up.

Plus, I think it's actually healthy to have a certain amount of unpredictability in every situation, a little brokenness or tenderness. I hate it in the moment. It drives me crazy. But I'm sure it keeps me cautious and aware as I move forward. This is good. Furthermore, it helps me keep growing, never totally relying on myself, and never sitting around waiting for all the answers.

So, when I don't get the answers I want, I keep moving. I've made mistakes doing that. I've also had a few victories. I know God can do something with my good moves, and he can even do something with the bad ones; but he can't do much with no movement at all.

I try to decide and progress. That's the best I can do. He'll have to take care of the rest.

Checking for Updates

Once I've decided to keep moving, I ask for further direction, further guidance.

Years ago, while I was still at my office job, an "opportunity" came my way to buy and develop ten acres of land. I put together a plan to build homes on it. The project was a little beyond my experience and budget, but I was willing to take the risk since the area was really growing. My wife and I talked extensively about it, and I had her full support. We figured we could make it about two years financially before the project needed to begin generating income from the home sales. And while I managed the project, I could write my book on the side.

I prayed. There was no answer. But it was a good, realistic plan, and we went for it. I left my office job, we moved our family to the area, and we started to put together this new life. We were *all in*.

Along the way, I asked God for guidance and the ability to know what decisions were good or bad. I hired professionals to compensate in areas where I was deficient. I had a site developer, architect, builder, accountant, lawyer, mortgage broker, and realtor. I had meetings with various governmental boards and departments.

I kept praying and moving along as time and money flowed into the project.

The startup months went well. I had momentum. It felt good and right. But then things started to slow down and get difficult.

There were zoning issues. The state's department of transportation wanted to widen the road bordering the property, which would take away land and reduce the number of lots for homes. That meant a smaller profit margin. I had second thoughts. Was this project still worth the increased risk? So, I prayed more.

I was making all the right contacts and doing everything I could. But I wasn't getting answers I needed from the governmental authorities. The project was stalled. I kept praying about what to do next to get the ball rolling. But it wouldn't. It was becoming a dead end. I was losing money, and it looked like I would only lose more.

Eventually, I decided to pull out. It just didn't make sense to continue. The time and money I invested were gone—about half a year's salary.

I thought God had failed me, and I was angry with him. Why didn't he give me more ideas on how to solve the problems? Why didn't he open more doors?

Looking back, I can see how that project would have been my grave. It would have ruined our lives. It was just too ambitious at our stage in life. And it would have consumed all my time.

I didn't see that back then, in the heat of the moment and raw emotions. But God saw it.

Couldn't he have stopped us earlier? I suppose. But then I wouldn't have learned to be more cautious when gambling with our finances. This failed pursuit was the best way to learn some critical life lessons. If God had spared me that pain, I could have really screwed up our lives. Where would that have put my dreams and our overall goals?

God knew best.

Your Shopping Cart Has [1] Item

When I'm not praying for a specific response or guidance, I'm praying for something in particular that I want.

Like a baby.

My wife and I spent most of the first years of our marriage fighting, but when things got a little more stable, we decided to start trying to have kids. Like many couples, we started praying for a baby. Within six months, our prayers were answered, and we were ecstatic.

Within the first few weeks of finding out, we picked out two different color schemes for the baby's room (depending on the gender of course), we called or emailed every breathing person we knew about our news, we went through what must have been 100,000 baby names, and we began our list of all the baby items we would need. We were having so much fun. Each day seemed better than the one before.

The doctor visits went well. Everything was right on track, and soon we'd have an ultrasound picture of the little fluttering bean in her belly.

Before the pregnancy, my wife had scheduled a trip with a friend. When the time for it came, we wondered if flying was safe for her, so we called the doctor. At that stage, you worry about everything; you'll scarcely let your wife eat pepper if you think it might harm the baby. But the human body is amazing, and the doctor said the planned trip was fine.

She went with her friend and had an amazing time. On the way home, she called me from an airport layover. She was upset, and I could barely make out what she was saying. She had started bleeding. I reassured her everything would be fine and told her to get on the plane and just come home. I reminded her of what the doctor said. I also mentioned how the same thing happened with some of our friends, and it turned out okay. I picked her up at the airport and told her I'd scheduled a doctor's appointment for the next morning.

In the doctor's office, everything seemed fine. We were so relieved, and we went on planning our new lives. The fun was back. We were getting even more excited, because after one more doctor's visit we'd get that ultrasound picture, and maybe even be able to faintly hear that fluttering little heart. But a few days later we got a phone call reporting the results of her full blood tests. Something was wrong. We'd lost the baby.

What can be said about these situations? Our hearts ached. My wife blamed herself. "I knew the trip was a bad idea," she said. "It's my fault." This went on for weeks.

There was the anger to deal with as well. We were praying for something good—but we were let down.

Honestly, I'm still not sure what to take from that experience. I don't know why it happened. I know, however, that it changed me. These types of experiences have a way of doing that. People either become worse—jaded, mad, and bitter—or they become better— more mature, stronger, more appreciative of life.

It took time, but this experience made both of us better. It stretched and deepened us personally and spiritually. Pain is a very effective teacher. I hope we never experience that again, and I wouldn't wish it on anyone. In fact, I hope bad stuff never happens again to anyone anywhere. But that's not reality. Not yet anyway. We live in a broken world where bad things happen. If we're willing, however, we can become stronger people and grow through the pain.

I still pray for stuff I want. I just pray a little differently. I ask God for it, but I also ask for the strength and wisdom to get through whatever may come. And I also pray that I don't stay mad at him too long if things don't work out like I want.

Again, it helps me in this to view God as that perfect father. I picture him as caring, understanding, and helping me through these times.

Maybe he's saying something like this:

"Jason, I know this can all be extremely difficult and taxing on your soul. That's not how I meant life to be, but that's how things turned out. One day everything will be okay. I promise you'll make it through. Sometimes that will be because I give you a direct boost. I'll literally fill you with my Spirit and give you my strength. You'll know it, because you'll feel it.

"But sometimes you'll have to get that boost in a more indirect way. Sometimes I need to let you go through stuff so you get stronger as a person. That's the most valuable boost you could ever have, because with it you'll be a better person next time around. You'll learn to be patient and content, no matter what comes your way. You'll learn to be thankful for what you have; your happiness won't hinge on what you want or get.

"I'm trying to help you as much as I can to be better at life itself, considering the state of the world as you know it. Ultimately, that's what I really want for you, my child."

Reply To: me@myselfandI.me

So, I pray for answers, for guidance, and for stuff. But the most unselfish, benevolent, and healthy kind of praying I do is the kind I tend to do the least.

It's when I pray for others. You know the type of prayers: help my brother pass his bar exam, let my friend get that job so he can pay the bills, heal that person's cancer, let my neighbor come to his senses and come back to his family, give my kids wisdom to make good decisions, etc.

Do these prayers for others "work"? The answer to that is seen primarily in how my experience of prayer affects me as an individual.

I've concluded that this is ultimately what praying is all about.

What I want for myself gets in the way of praying for others. It's so easy to become self-absorbed. I'm always on my mind, so I don't often think of others. Reminding myself to pray for them helps me step outside my own little world and get a more sober view of myself.

Don't we all know people who are totally self-absorbed? Lonely? Bitter? Cutting out people so they won't have to risk being hurt? I know I am someone who could easily evolve into the worst version of me by doing this.

I am tempted to end relationships when they start to inconvenience me. And since every relationship gets inconvenient at times, I want to end them all in some form or fashion. I could easily turn into the type of person that moves from marriage to marriage as I focus on changing others rather than myself.

As I devolved and ruined my family, I probably wouldn't let anyone speak into my life—to bounce ideas back and forth, to make suggestions, to encourage, or to challenge. I would only care about my own view, and would expect others to agree with it.

Most of my thinking would be about what I wanted and what I needed. Sadly, this would only make me worse as a person, not better.

For me, praying is one of the best antidotes to these temptations. Praying for others helps me be less self-consumed. That's why this type of praying is the most important. And it works.

Please Wait While Your Call Is Redirected

I've decided praying is a lot like gravity. It's there, and it's always doing something, even if it isn't exactly what you want or expect.

I first learned about gravity at age five when I jumped off a roof and jammed both my knees. It was painful. It took days for the soreness to go away. What was I doing on a roof at age five? That's another story about growing up in a single-parent home with little supervision in a white-trash neighborhood.

I recently had it out with my dad. It was time. I was carrying thirty years of baggage. I told him off good too. I felt he had it coming.

My father never let me stay inside as a kid. He always made me go outside and play. He said it wasn't healthy to sit around eating chips and watching TV all the time, which is what I wanted to do (and what I do now as an adult). So, I grew up climbing trees and riding bikes—getting cuts, bumps, and bruises.

He didn't give me many of the things I wanted either. I wanted a black Huffy Pro-Thunder bike with yellow mag wheels. What I got was a blue bike with spokes. It was still pretty nice; I could pop wheelies and jump ramps just fine.

He also made me work. I think I was five when he started letting me pick up around the job sites and earn some money. Money was never a gift from him; I always had to work for it. He said things weren't free in life, and you had to work and earn what you wanted, "or else you won't appreciate it."

He disciplined me too. I learned very young not to talk back. He wasn't afraid to give me a whack when I needed it, and I needed it a lot.

All these things—every single one of them—I *hated* at the time. But you know, he was right. (And I told him so and thanked him in that recent conversation where I had it out with him.) I'm glad he didn't give me everything I wanted. I appreciate it now as an adult, since I have a different perspective. It's a perspective I'm starting to understand more and apply as I pray.

As I've tried to understand if prayer works, I keep realizing that my father-view is key. If I can somehow keep picturing God as the perfect father, that brings it all together for me.

God, as a loving father, may not answer every prayer, like the prayer of the lazy student who hasn't studied for her final, but she's asking God to help her pass the class.

Or consider whose prayer gets answered first in this scenario: the tipsy driver who's praying he won't get caught by the cops or the family on the same highway that is asking God to get them home safely?

God may not need to give further guidance to the woman who's praying about whether to marry a guy she's been dating. He has a reputation for cheating, he sports a prison record, and he drives a black van with a jumping unicorn airbrushed on one side and a wizard with a crystal ball on the other. The answer to her prayer should be obvious (as it already is to everyone who knows her). What further guidance can she possibly need?

I think a lot of the time we tend to make a mess of things and then come to God in prayer, expecting him to clean it all up. Sometimes he will. But sometimes we have to bear the consequences of our decisions.

Sometimes he has other reasons for not answering our prayers. Or he answers them in ways we don't understand at the moment.

I've learned that unanswered prayers aren't necessarily no's from God. Many times, it's a "no for now," and in time, it may become a yes, after I grow a little. And every so often, his answer is a yes right away.

Actually, I think we all get a lot more yes answers from God than we recognize. We just don't notice them as much. I think I'm entitled to the perfectly happy little life, and I get mad when I don't have it. As a result, I have a habit of not saying thank you very often to God. But in reality, how many of my prayers have already been answered? I have an amazing wife, beautiful kids, a job, a house, and my health. Those are all big screaming *yes* answers that I take for granted every day.

So I'm starting to think prayer works *every* time and *all* the time, to some degree.

The real point of praying, I think, is that it draws me closer to God. So if I'm at least doing it, it's working.

Occasionally, my wife and I have it out. I hate it. It feels so undone. No matter how much we talk, we don't understand or agree with each other's perspective. But in the end, we have to agree to move past that. Investing in our relationship doesn't always mean we totally agree or both get what we want. More often, it means we reconcile and walk away in unity, having communicated our honest differences, and deciding to progress forward together. Sometimes that's the best proof of our bond. It's easy to strengthen and walk in unity in the relationship when all is well and we totally agree and we both get what we want. But the true test is when we stick with each other in the midst of strain and unmet expectations.

In the same way, praying isn't all about me and what I want. If that's how I approach prayer—if that's what I expect from it or think it's for—it won't work.

Prayer is supposed to change me more than it changes the circumstances around me. It turns my heart toward God. It helps me focus less on myself. And it puts me in a place to be touched, guided, and comforted.

God isn't out of the office or out of touch. He's there waiting. Sometimes we need to just be "on hold" for a while.

#3 The Bible

One of my uncles is a naval architect. He's brilliant. He was leading a successful company by the time he was twenty-two. Today people fly him all around the world to tap into his expertise. He has converted cargo ships into cruise ships, he's cut cruise ships in half, and he's expanded cruise ships to twice their size.

Like I said, he's smart.

Numbers and equations don't bother my uncle, but math scares me to death. I used to love it, but something ruined that. It was called college algebra. After three D's, I adjusted my major to something that didn't require those hard numbers and formulas.

I have a tendency to give up on things I don't understand or are too confusing.

Don't get me wrong, I'm happy not being brilliant. Have you ever known someone who's brilliant? A true intellectual? A real genius? I've known a few. Although they're brilliant people, they've had plenty of personal deficiencies and were a little odd. Intellectuals seem to wear styles from twenty-five years ago, have bad hygiene, and constantly lose their keys. Geniuses do things like drop off their dry cleaning with credit cards and money still in the pockets. They're often disorganized to a legendary degree and are amazingly bad drivers. They have poor social skills, but that doesn't bother them because they're elitists too. They should be filthy rich due to their smarts, but for some reason they're not.

So, I'm perfectly content not being too smart.

My philosophy is that I want to be just smart enough to enjoy life. I want enough common sense to make decent decisions most of the time, choices I can at least live with. I want to be able to look back and see at least a 51 percent good-decision average. Some might say that's aiming low. Or if you knew me, you might say I'm dreaming. But at least this average has forward momentum and would keep me confident and motivated enough to try new challenges.

So, it doesn't bother me that much that I'm not too good at math. I know enough to get by. If not, I use a calculator.

But there's still that other trait I mentioned, my old habit of giving up. It's not one of my finer qualities. There are days when it's just easier to give up than to go through the difficult process of forcing myself to wrap my mind around something unfamiliar or something I don't like. Giving up doesn't build my character or improve my quality of life. It has often gotten me off track, keeping *better* from becoming *best* or preventing *good* from growing into *great*. I know I've robbed myself of hope, contentment, and opportunity many times by giving up.

Giving up looks fine in the heat of a moment, but it does

eventually yield regret.

From what I can tell, every situation or endeavor will eventually bring a sort of dip in the road. This is where the giving up has its greatest appeal. It brings the illusion of a change that may feel positive, simply because it's something different. But giving up like this is going backward, and it always will be.

As I continued on my Christian journey, I took a Bible with me. It's the primary tool for just such an excursion. In fact, I read it all the way through a couple times in the first year or so after I decided to try following God actively. But I stumbled upon some problems. The darn thing wasn't working right.

It was like not having a can opener on a camping trip in the outback. I wanted what was inside the can, and I needed it; I knew it could sustain me. But I just couldn't get to it.

I was tempted to just throw the Bible in the trash and burn it, but that seemed wrong. So, I just put it on the shelf until I needed it again.

I hate that the Bible seemed too hard to reconcile with real life. I hate that it sometimes left me more confused than if I'd just left it on the shelf. I was trying to combine my experience with the information I found there, and the mix wasn't working. More and more, the Bible seemed old, boring, hard to understand, and even harder to relate to my day-to-day life.

I hit a dip and started hating the Bible.

Actually, forget the dip. I hit a wall.

Y = ?

I used to carry a Bible in high school. It certainly didn't make me more popular. Being a Christian wasn't cool, and carrying a Bible was even goofier. It brought me a few more nicknames than other classmates. Bible Thumper was the most common.

Thankfully, life went on. But I bet those kids making fun of me would be happy to know I soon "thumped" less enthusiastically.

I have a natural tendency to question the credibility of the Bible. Can it be trusted? Can I still wholeheartedly pursue the faith I hold to be true, the faith that's built on these words, stories, and teachings? Why would I? Why should I?

I started to wonder if the Bible was nothing more than the tool of rich and powerful white guys in the past that refined it to fit their personal agendas (you know, to suppress other ethnic groups and women) and maintain their status quo.

Or was it just the record and musings of a bunch of beatniks smoking dope and writing their hallucinations down? That's what some people say about the Bible, and it's hard not to believe it when you're having your own doubts. There seems to be so much you have to overlook in order to believe it. I hate that I can't figure it all out.

In more optimistic moments, I've tried sharing some of the truths I've learned from the Bible, but this seems to highlight the problem even more. There's an awkward tension, as if I'm trying to explain the plot of some obscure cult classic movie like *Blade Runner:* "No really, Harrison Ford is *also* a Replicant! He's not even human, but you have to see the director's cut to totally get it." (That's not true. The director's cut is even more confusing.)

I hate feeling like I'm trying to convince people to believe the Bible, because I'm not always totally convinced myself. I don't want them to end up like me, even more discouraged than before they started their journeys. Still, deep down inside, I feel the Bible is somehow good and true.

Eventually, I decided not to give up. I wanted to turn this over a little more and figure out if I could really believe and trust the Bible.

The first step for me was to decide how to approach the Bible and then to understand what it is.

Right Angle

It's taken a long time, and I've had to ease off from the absolutism of my youth. That's not to say I stopped believing in absolute truth, but back then I wanted to understand *everything* in the Bible, and I wouldn't be satisfied with anything less. I thought that was the only way it could be believable.

But who can understand everything about anything? I'd accepted my limitations in understanding math, but it was trickier with the Bible, supposedly a book of truth.

To resolve this predicament, I determined I needed to strike a balance somewhere. Not a mindset of compromise, but looking at the Bible with a balanced, common sense approach. I wanted to become confident enough about it and familiar enough with it to glean wisdom for everyday life. Even though I couldn't understand everything in the Bible, it could still be useful, helpful, and inspirational.

Once I approached the Bible with that mindset, everything began to change.

Still, I had to overcome confusion over what the Bible is. I treated it like a book of answers meets an owner's manual—something to "use" for my life. This was wrong, and wrong comparisons lead to incorrect assumptions and inaccurate expectations.

For example, if you try to argue the merits of rock music over classical or a bicycle over a motorcycle or winter over summer, it doesn't really work. It's an effort in futility. Trying to totally resolve an inequitable comparison will fail every time, because it builds on a false premise—that there's absolute equivalence between two completely different ideas. Mismatched comparisons create unfair tension. It's no different when it comes to the Bible.

It seems like a lot of people run into this problem with the Bible. School boards and parents are frequently tied up in this friction. It manifests itself in the supposed conflict between the Bible and science, as parents try to get the biblical record of creation into science classes. That's an argument that can never be won, because it's a comparison problem.

I understand science as the combination of theory and empirical research. Scientific theories are formulated on that basis or should be. The Bible isn't science. The Bible doesn't belong in a science class based on those principles. It's like arguing music theory against architecture. The Bible isn't meant to be formulaic in nature or sliced so precisely. It's not based on scientific theory and cannot be tested like science is. That's not the fault of the Bible. It just doesn't belong in the same category as a science book.

As a parent, I understand the need to try to resolve this argument in a free society that's supposed to be based on the unbiased exploration of a multitude of ideas. The Bible really picks up where science leaves off. When science is honest and admits it can't totally explain the origins of the universe, perhaps certain biblical ideas deserve a brief mention. When theories of origins are discussed in a science class, perhaps this philosophy can be touched on. I think every good scientist should be a little bit of a philosopher. If the argument from parents is in this context, I get it.

Either way, the Bible's not a book of science.

So, what kind of book is it?

Actually, the Bible's not a book at all. It's a collection of separate works—sixty-six of them from forty different authors, written in different languages in different times and cultures, and geared toward different audiences for different reasons. The collection includes historical records, letters, poetry, songs, stories, standards, and philosophy.

But knowing that still wasn't enough for me. I still felt quite inadequate when I read it. And who wants to sit around reading and feeling like a half-wit? I just wanted to learn more about the Bible and grow in my understanding of it.

I eventually found some tools to help me.

Rational Expressions

Old, boring, and busted. If you ever need help sleeping, just read the Bible. It's wordy and you'll get cranky after a few paragraphs; at least I do. That is, if I'm reading certain translations with words like *thee, thou,* and *thine* in them. They make me hate reading it all over again.

No, the Bible wasn't originally written in Old English, or any kind of English. (And Jesus probably didn't have blonde hair and blue eyes either, but that's another subject.) The Bible we read was translated into English from a variety of ancient tongues.

Translating it requires sensitivity to the original languages and the cultures, as is always true with translation. Any creditable translator worth his weight in words is especially loyal to *context* (the surrounding circumstances that influence a particular piece of writing) and true to the *syntax* (rules and principles about word order, sentence structure, and grammar). He wants to be faithful to the original intent as he tries to communicate it in a way that makes sense to the modern reader.

I know firsthand this is no easy task. My father is from Sweden, straight off the boat. In his early twenties, he and some friends decided to take a leisurely sail across the English Channel to the U.K., then across to France, then back to Sweden. I suppose they were retracing some ancient Viking pillaging routes. Long story short, they had so much fun on their trip they kept going, and two years later ended up in Fort Lauderdale, Florida. My dad never moved back to Sweden, and here I am.

I was born in the U.S.A., as Springsteen sang, but I speak Swedish fluently. It really doesn't come in too handy, though it's not like I don't try to use it. Every once in a while I hear some tourists speaking Swedish, and it's always fun to listen in. I casually hover nearby hoping to catch an insult or lie so I can give them the shakedown. It's never happened.

I'm keenly aware some things don't translate easily between English and Swedish. For example, if I took a visiting cousin to experience the great American pastime of baseball, my skills could come in handy when he wanted to make the experience complete by purchasing a hot dog. Before yelling to the vendor, he first tells me in Swedish what he wants to communicate: *"Jag vilja en varm korv!"* I'd never tell him to call out the literal translation: "I want a warm sausage!" It would bring funny looks or trouble from the guys next to us who are slamming back beers. So, I skillfully consider context, syntax, and intent, and tell him to holler, *"Haya Buddee, vun hawte dawhga ovurr heeeri!"* (In Swedish twang, that's "Hey Buddy, one hot dog over here!") Then all goes well at the big game. Go Braves!

It's funny, in translating between Swedish and English, I have the urge not to give up on either language. I try harder to make it understandable. In fact, I get a headache sometimes when trying to speak Swedish as I translate my English thoughts. It would be even more difficult if I tried to translate Swedish from several hundred years ago. To be accurate I would have to patiently study old books, art, history, traditions, and other cultural aspects. It could be done. It has been done. But not by me.

Two tools really help me with this kind of thing when I read the Bible. First, I've picked a specific English translation that fits me, since I can't read the Bible's original languages. I was surprised how many English versions are available. There's quite a range.

The more literal translations will track parallel to the original mechanics of the original language. But they can be quite wooden in how they read. I find a literal translation hard to track with, and I lose interest. But literal translations can be good because you decide for yourself how to interpret and apply what you're reading. It just takes more work and good study tools and reference books.

Literal translations include the *King James Version* (KJV) from the early 1600s, *Young's Literal Translation* (YLT) from the 1800s, and the *English Standard Version* (ESV) from 2001, as well as various editions of what's called an "interlinear" Bible (which is the most literal).

I used to be militant about reading the KJV. Maybe you've met people like that. I'd been told I had to read the KJV because nothing else was God-inspired. That may well be the main reason I started hating the Bible. If you don't know what's going on, the KJV might just drive you mad.

All this arguing over translations is stupid. For centuries, followers of God didn't even have the luxury of a Bible accessible to every person. And somehow the Christian faith survived. Maybe it's time to put this argument to rest. But if literal is what you want in your studies, I've found an interlinear Bible to be the most useful. It's very straightforward and literal in converting the original texts.

Other translations are really paraphrases, and they consider our modern context more. Some take great liberty in this area when interpreting, as they try to use very plain or contemporary language. They may even have current cuss words and slang expressions to make their points. They're good if you're just sitting down to read the Bible like you would a novel. The flow is better and they're easier to understand. They can even be humorous at times, which always helps a story move along.

Some examples of paraphrased translations, all from recent decades, are the *New Living Translation* (NLT), *The Message,* and the *Good News Bible* (GNB).

I like to land somewhere in the middle between a literal version and a paraphrase.

The right translation helps me not doze, but it also helps me stay in the original context enough to preserve the meaning. It just makes sense. Right now I'm reading a translation called the *New Century Version* (NCV). I absolutely love it. Another one that's good is *Today's New International Version* (TNIV).

Sometimes I also use a Bible dictionary when I read (*Holman's Bible Dictionary* is a good one). This will define confusing words or terms when I am caught up. I also highly recommend *Halley's Bible Handbook*. It's cheap, small, and portable. More importantly, it's comprehensive and concise at the same time and easy to follow. Along with a good translation, it will definitely help you get off on the right foot reading the Bible.

Mainly, when I read the Bible, I just want to be able to make sense of it and be able to carry a thought through to the everyday. I guess I'm trying to give the Bible the similar respect I give Swedish and English.

So maybe knowing an obscure second language has helped me after all. *Tack så mycket, Pappa!*

Variables

Why's it called cheesecake? Isn't it really more like pie, with the consistency and the crust? But I guess "cheese pie" just doesn't sound appealing.

Then there are buildings. If you step in an elevator and want to go to the second story, you press "1." So, in reality, a ten-story building actually has eleven floors.

And why do people answer their phones and then say, "I can't talk right now, I'll call you back"? Just let it go to voicemail you blockhead!

I sit here wondering about contradictions with cheesecake and elevators—but hey, they have nothing on the Bible.

Even after using my strategy and tools, I've found some thematic challenges in the Bible. They hit me like a cold shower.

There are two examples that come to mind when I think of this issue.

The first contradiction I hit was *murder.* How dare God tell me not to murder in one of his Ten Commandments and then tell someone else in the Bible to take another's life! What the heck is that? For example, God told King Saul (Israel's first king) to kill the Amalekites. Why would God do that?

I kept reading and researching, trying to figure it out. I was blistering mad that I caught God in a trap. But as I read, I realized how important it is to remember that there's not a lot of similarity between how we live today and how civilizations lived thousands of years ago. It's a bit of a stretch to evaluate social and civil justice from so long ago by our standards today. Even in this country, how we lived a hundred years ago was very different.

Many people in the past were fighting to just survive each day. They had to get by without our modern marvels. They wrestled against the elements, nature, and other people. Justice and responsibility were often dealt with immediately within the community or tribe. So, the context of their lives was quite different. Recognizing this helped me make sense of this issue.

While I was wrestling with justice in the Bible, there was an abduction and murder of a child named Adam Walsh still fresh in the minds of people in South Florida (where I lived at the time). His dad, John Walsh, had just started the show *America's Most Wanted* in order to catch criminals. And it was working. It got me thinking that there might be a difference between murder and killing.

I didn't have a family back then, but I knew if something like that happened to my child, I would probably take drastic action. If someone broke into my house, tied up my family, and held us hostage with guns, I would feel no hesitation in trying to break free and defend my family, to the death if necessary. Although this could mean killing, it wouldn't be murder—a premeditated action with no justification. In contrast, if my neighbor made me mad and I planned to take his life, just waiting for the right time, that would be murder. So, to me, murder is always killing, but killing isn't always murder, especially in defense of the innocent.

Back to King Saul and the Amalekites. After more reading, I discovered the Amalekites had waged unprovoked attacks on Israel on many occasions. So, in the context of the time, I could see God allowing King Saul to take action against the Amalekites in defense of the Hebrews for the protection of their families. That just didn't seem so savage anymore.

So, I stuck with the Bible a little, and God became a little bigger again. I saw how he often encouraged the Hebrews to maintain peaceful relationships with surrounding nations and cultures. Here was diplomacy, civility, and responsibility—not killing. Unfortunately, there were times when hard actions were unavoidable, for justice to take its course in a more primitive context.

The next contradiction that bothered me was the lack of worthiness on the part of people God tended to bless. They were less than perfect most of the time. For example, although God commanded monogamy in the Bible, he still maintained a close relationship with individuals like King David and King Solomon, who had multiple wives. If polygamy was so wrong, why didn't God cut them off? Why did he give them honor and wisdom and continue to talk to them? These kings certainly knew better.

But for them, polygamy was a sign of status and power, though it brought more headaches than they thought it would. If you read their writings, you'll learn that by the end of their lives, they regretted their many bad decisions (like polygamy). That helped me see what God was doing.

God loves humanity and wants to establish a relationship with us, no matter what. He doesn't expect us to be perfect. That's what I learned from this apparent inconsistency. He wasn't approving their bad behavior. Instead, he was accepting *them,* telling them they needed to change, and still loving them. This reaffirmed God's character for me again, which is what drew me to him in the first place.

I learned it all over again: God doesn't require me to be perfect in order to establish a relationship with me. Jesus doesn't either. He wants a willing heart. God is as patient with me as he was with David and Solomon.

In this process, I also found more helpful tools. I used various commentaries on the Bible. I bought about a dozen, because I wanted as much information as I could get on these issues. I wanted to compare all the varying viewpoints so I could decide for myself. And I did.

This opened my eyes. The Bible's a true record of God's interactions with people he loves, people who can be both brilliant and idiotic. All the ugly details are there of the relationship he has with humanity, because authentic relationships are messy. It's all there in unapologetic glory. The Bible doesn't hide anything.

Figuring out these contradictions and using these tools has also made the Bible less boring. It can be weird, confusing, interesting, exciting, and inspiring all at the same time. Like *General Hospital* meets *Indiana Jones* meets *Lord of the Rings* meets *Monty Python*. It's filled with stories of action, adventure, fighting, sex, love, and humor. There are even fire-breathing dragons and a talking donkey. But no ogre. (Sorry, Shrek.)

Square Root

The Bible's old. Sometimes old stuff makes my eyes roll. Like when the old-timer starts to reminisce and offer wisdom: "Back in my day…" And he proceeds to tell us young whippersnappers how they had to walk five miles to and from school—uphill both ways and wearing no shoes. Somehow, things were simpler and harder all at the same time back then.

Let's be honest. Something in all of us wants to respond, "Yeah, right, give me a break, Grandpa! I love you, but I'm too cool and with-it to believe that stuff."

There's something in me that gives less credibility to somebody or something old, which I don't think is a particularly good reaction. In many ancient cultures, age was revered and elders were held in high regard. Today it's a little different. I think it's partly unavoidable. So many people have grown up in broken homes, how are they supposed to embrace traditional family values like commitment, devotion, sacrifice, and loyalty? Plus, our consumer mindset leads us to always want the newest and latest innovations and developments.

We've grown up culturally to question anything that's established or an accepted norm. As a result, what's old seems irrelevant and less credible. We buck against traditions and distrust old wisdom. But that is reckless.

Not that questioning the old isn't sometimes positive. Challenging the status quo is at the root of every new discovery. Breakthroughs come by thinking outside the box or swimming against the current. But the most helpful new developments also build on the past rather than discard everything from it.

When I was growing up, when it came to reports and projects at school, there was one resounding credible source: *Encyclopedia Britannica*. There was no Internet then; we had to actually get up out of our chairs and go to something known as a "library" to do research. Every single kid cited the *Encyclopedia Britannica* as his or her main source. Everyone trusted it blindly. No teacher of mine ever questioned information gleaned from it.

But that trust wouldn't have been there if, for example, we had only the first edition of *Encyclopedia Britannica* from way back in the 1700s. An encyclopedia exists to offer *information,* and that information has to be constantly updated as discoveries and changes are made in science, history, culture, etc.

But what about the Bible? Is it merely informational and, therefore, needing to be updated with the times?

I realized that the Bible was more than informational. It was also meant to be *inspirational*. So, I learned to think differently about it being old.

The Bible's not a record of research like an encyclopedia. After many years of reading the Bible, I've concluded that its primary purpose is to communicate moral and spiritual truths through things like history, poetry, songs, prophecy, and parables. It tells the story of the Creator bringing healing to a broken world throughout the ages. It's a story of redemption for souls, initiated and completed by God through Jesus.

As much as I get annoyed that principles in the Bible compel me to thrust myself into the gray areas, I don't think it needs to evolve or be updated with the times. I don't think moral and spiritual truths should evolve. What evolves is our understanding of them or our desire to apply them. When the Bible says something old-fashioned—like don't sleep around, don't lie, or don't take what doesn't belong to you—that doesn't make it any less believable to me. It just means I might be getting mad at the standard it challenges me with.

So, I try to be okay with the Bible being old and what that tells me about myself.

Law of Probability

When I was a kid, a standard joke line was "Who's buried in Grant's tomb?" For some reason most kids would say they didn't know; the obvious was too obvious.

But maybe we weren't so dumb after all. It's widely accepted—and never questioned, as far as I know—that Ulysses Grant is entombed there, but do we really know that? There are no eyewitnesses alive today, no home videos of the ceremony, no reality TV footage to help prove it. Even the excavated bones would be of little help, since there's no DNA record to match them with. And even if all this evidence existed, and someone examined and verified it, could we believe that person without a doubt? The only way to prove something is to see it unfold for yourself, but you still face the challenge of proving it to others who didn't actually see it for themselves. Why would they believe *you?* Are you a trustworthy person?

Truly, seeing is believing. But we just can't see *everything.* So, nothing can be proven one way or another. One can only hope to build evidence to that effect. That's what everything comes down to.

When I mentioned I was Swedish, did you believe me? Why? I actually can't prove to you I'm Swedish. Sure, I could show you where Sweden is on the map. I could describe my visits there. I could tell you about Swedish traditions and the brutal history of the Vikings. I could even call my dad and let you talk to him so you could hear his sing-songy accent. I could let you listen while he and I speak to each other in Swedish. But all that wouldn't actually *prove* anything. It simply uses evidence to build a case, like lawyers do.

I can also make authentic Swedish meatballs. So, am I Swedish? *Yumpin' yimini,* you decide.

As much as I want it to be otherwise, the Bible's trustworthiness and accuracy can't be proven. Yes, I hated finally admitting that, but there's no easy solution to explain it away. The best that can be done is to offer evidence to build the case. That's the only "proof" there is for the entire content of the Bible. Obviously, none of us today were witnesses to the events it relates or personally knew the people involved. There's just no way to substantiate everything in it. However, I have learned some things about the Bible that build a case for its creditability and help me trust it more.

First, let me briefly deal with a portion of the Bible called the Old Testament. It's everything in the Bible that was written before Jesus was born. It's essentially the Jewish Bible, and Hebrews call it the *Tanakh*.

Over the centuries, Jewish rabbis and scholars had to reproduce by hand the copies of the Old Testament that we base our translations on today. Many people might view this as a liability—as evidence for the possibility for manipulation. But with a little research, I discovered the opposite is truer. The Scriptures were viewed as holy and sacred and not to be tampered with.

The work of copying the Scriptures was an honor, and only those of the highest character, gifting, and training were chosen for this rigorous and tedious task. Still, they were only human, so they had to take special care to avoid mistakes. A scribe doing this work was allowed to make a maximum of only three small errors, or else *all* his work was destroyed. In this case, an entire year of work would be totally wasted.

The New Testament we have today shares a similar reputation for accuracy, but it came about in a different way. Many of the "books" in the New Testament are actually letters written by leaders appointed personally by Jesus. They contain encouragement and instruction for the earliest Christians that wanted to know as much as possible about Jesus and his teachings. So, when a group of followers received one of these letters, it was very special. It was quickly and frequently copied, and the copies spread like wildfire. It's like they were forwarding all the emails they could about him to all their friends and family.

This had far-reaching implications. The world as we know it has been unmistakably affected by the teachings of Jesus, and this is largely credited to the passion of these early followers who spread these truths around.

There are tens of thousands of copies and fragments from these letters today. When compared to each other, they're consistent to a supernatural degree. This also points to quite an attention to accuracy by those responsible for copying and maintaining these documents.

Many people assume that over time, the Bible must have been changed or diluted in what it contains. But the evidence indicates that the Bible's accuracy is much more verifiable than any other ancient written work. For example, the Greek philosopher Plato died around 347 BC, but the earliest copy of his writings goes back only to AD 900 — some 1,200 years after he actually penned or spoke the words — and these earliest copies of his works include only seven full or partial manuscripts. By contrast, the various parts of the New Testament were written between 60 and 100 AD, and the oldest partial copy is dated only about twenty-five years later. Plus, there are approximately 24,000 full and partial copies altogether of the ancient Greek New Testament. That's quite impressive.

To me, the Bible should be the gold standard for accuracy in ancient writings. Many people dispute its reliability, but most people who make these objections to me admit they've never actually pursued the subject or even read the Bible.

Was the Bible manipulated to spread propaganda? That seems unlikely when you consider how the Bible includes so many ugly details about people who claim to follow God. People like King David, the prophet Samuel, and the apostle Peter certainly don't always come across looking good, and that would seem to reflect poorly on God. If I were trying to persuade people through propaganda, I'd leave out details that tarnish my reputation. Wouldn't you?

A Factor of X

The most outrageous issue I had with the Bible is that it seems like one giant *X-File*. It contains signs, wonders, and miracles, and it's built on events and circumstances that are totally unimaginable, unexplainable, and supernatural. There's creation, angels, demons, splitting seas, Adam and Eve, a super-strong man, a ten-foot giant, armies of hundreds defeating armies of thousands, a giant fish who swallows some dude who lives to tell about it, blind people seeing, lame people walking, dead people rising, and a man walking on water. And let's not forget God the Creator, Jesus his Son, and the devil.

To believe all this stuff, I felt like I had to remove my brain and insert mush. If only I had help from Fox Mulder, on the case with Dana Scully (keeping him accountable), scouring the world for the truth.

It's no wonder the Bible's put in the same category with UFO sightings, the Loch Ness monster, and Bigfoot. I heard a gentleman on a radio talk show say that the Bible is "obviously myth and must be considered a work of fiction." He said we must all come to terms with the idea that religion in general is untrue and must be put aside for the sake of reason and enlightenment.

I understand the difficulty in reconciling reason and faith. The Bible contains supernatural elements that are unbelievable and unexplainable by their very nature. And it should, if you ask me, since it's about God. If there were a God, wouldn't things get supernatural when he gets involved? That's something I had to accept when I decided to live with faith. I hate it, but I accept it.

Calculating the Equation

For me it was a choice of trusting one of two theories. The first holds that the Bible is the product of corrupt, power-hungry men and their own agendas. They wanted to control and subdue the masses. They fed the opiate of religion to the people.

Admittedly, I find this easier to accept. Cynicism seems intrinsically entrenched in my being. It's the environment and culture I grew up in and live in now.

But if these schemers wanted to conquer the wills and minds of the common folk, they didn't do a good job of manipulating and corrupting the Bible. In many respects, they were idiots at it, once all things are weighed and examined. They should have made the Bible more absolute and the people perfect.

I once heard a quote by George Orwell to the effect that some nonsense is so bad only an intellectual can believe it. So, I guess being average works to my advantage here. This theory of dishonest conspirators distorting the Bible just doesn't make much sense to me.

So, will I believe the harder theory? Could it be that this record was protected by stewards who preserved it—the bad and the good, the beauty and the horror—to keep it accurate? Could it be the Bible is an authentic collection of records of God's history with humankind? Of how much he endures and accepts? Of how much he loves us regardless?

In this multi-author, multi-book Bible, I see one theme shining through and connecting it all in a continuous thread down to its very last words. I've come to see that this book's not broken and doesn't need fixing; it's a story about fixing things that *have* been broken, especially the bond between God and humanity.

The Bible is tied together by one message. It is God loving humanity and wanting to rebuild a relationship that was lost. It provides old wisdom and new inspiration for a sometimes-lost soul like me.

My tendency to give up rather than work through stuff—and to get mad and want to walk away—creates a spiraling sense of hopelessness and gloom when it comes to matters of truth, purpose, and redemption (spiritual matters). But through my battles with the Bible, I've learned to give up less.

I still don't understand everything. I don't know everything. I don't agree with everything. I don't like everything. In fact, sometimes I still hate it.

I suppose I could make some hybrid of the two theories about the Bible that I find myself stuck between. I could decide which things in the Bible are right and which are not. In fact, I've tried this. The problem is, it creates a sliding standard. I end up not applying to my life even the parts in the Bible that are clear. When you're willing to rationalize and throw out some of it, it's easy to eventually discard all of it.

So, I choose to trust the Bible.

Unfortunately, the Bible hasn't helped me much with my math problem.

#4 Sin

I learned from my father how to buy the ugliest home in the neighborhood, renovate it yourself, and sell it for much more than you invested. You then buy another house in a little better neighborhood and start all over. When my wife and I bought our first house, we followed his example.

It was a little fixer-upper in a quaint neighborhood called Shady Banks, five miles from the beach in Fort Lauderdale. Sounds nice, doesn't it? The house was a dump, and not our first choice, but it made sense based on the location.

As is often the case, you never really know what you're getting into with a fixer-upper. I would start a task, and it would reveal another problem. I'd tackle that one, and another would present itself. Over time, I effectively touched every single square inch of every surface of that house. I exaggerate not. Interior walls, ceilings, floors, exterior walls, roof, and yard were all transformed through good, old-fashioned elbow grease. My blood, sweat, and tears singlehandedly increased that home's value.

In the process, I think we also singlehandedly drove up the stock price of Home Depot as we spent our savings there and then some. It was great when they advertised one of their big sales. I was all over it. I spent what seemed like a half a day there loading up. I finally jockeyed my carts into the checkout line. A dozen other anxious guys were behind me with similar loads.

After counting and scanning everything, the cashier totaled it up. I couldn't believe what I heard. I'd expected a total in the range of $600 to $800, depending on discounts. So, when the cashier told me $57, I was ecstatic. *I won! I beat Home Depot!*

I knew something wasn't right. But part of me wanted to ignore the internal prompts, hand over my credit card, pay, and be on my way.

I was suspended in time while a dialogue raged in my head. The battleground was heating up and the lines were drawn.

Good Jason: I should say something to the cashier.

Bad Jason: Why? It's not like you did anything wrong.

Good Jason: Sometimes it's just as wrong to *not* do something.

Bad Jason: Forget it! You don't have time to wait for her to correct it. After all, it's her fault. Besides, you spend tons of money here anyway.

Good Jason: Shut up! I'm trying to think here.

Bad Jason: You're making everyone behind you mad, you jerk. Let's get goin'!

Good Jason: Ringing it all up again won't take that long. Plus,

I'll sleep better.

Bad Jason: How about a Big Mac?

Good Jason: Don't try to distract me. But that does sound good. Maybe with a chocolate milkshake this time . . .

There I was, fighting with myself, about to sell my character for some free drywall and screws. Should I give up and give in? Was it really such a big deal?

We've all been there. Maybe it's tax season in a tough year, and we consider fudging the numbers a little. Or we're preparing a résumé to apply for a desperately needed job, and we're tempted to exaggerate some qualifications and stretch our experience a little. Not lies, of course— just a little creativity with the truth.

These moments reveal something about my character that I try to ignore. Some call it their bad sides, or alter egos. Dr. Jekyll called it Mr. Hyde. I just can't understand why I'm so easy to convince when it comes to doing something wrong. Bad habits catch on so much quicker than good ones. What's with that? I hate it, and I hate myself for it.

After giving in, I've often said things like, "Nobody's perfect," "I'm only human," "We all make mistakes." That makes it easier to disregard the fact that I've done something wrong or given in to evil. *Evil*—that's sounds so ugly. I suppose that's because it's a little too honest a description. How can I make these excuses and not hate myself even more?

Maybe saying this will make me think more responsibly and realize I may be hurting myself—or worse, hurting others. It makes me face the fact that I might be losing control, doing things I can't take back. I have to admit that doing wrong makes me feel guilty.

Then it becomes clear I have to work on changing. I definitely hate the work that goes with that. Changing is tough. And the difficult part is not forgetting my need for it.

Christianity doesn't help. Not at first, anyway. Jesus said things like, "I tell you the truth, everyone who lives in sin is a slave to sin."[1] He talks about weeding out "everything that causes sin and all who do evil."[2] In fact, I hate that term *sin*. So archaic. So direct.

I hate the fact that Christianity lays out standards and principles by which to weigh my sense of morality. It speaks of sin as missing the mark and doing something I know to be wrong. I can't ignore this, though everything in me wants to shout, *Just leave me alone!*

Under the Radar

Jesus is quite up-front about this evil in me, and I hate it. It adds yet another voice to my already annoying inner dialogue.

But I'm pretty stubborn. Sometimes I think the inside of my head would be a safe place to test the splitting of atoms, since my skull's so thick. I rebel against the idea of sin. Or I try to ignore it; I think it will go away if I take no notice. But for some reason this doesn't take away the guilt, and trying to ignore it gets harder and harder. I've learned that ignoring it is worse than just facing the facts.

I am rarely able to tame this dark force in me. It has an insatiable appetite, and my inclination toward it never seems to go away. The battle never ends. It's exhausting. But I've also figured out that victory will never be in sight until I turn and meet this predator. Whatever it is, whatever I call it, I have to admit it's real.

I'd never even thought about evil or its effects until my

Christianity challenged me on it. Who the heck wants to talk about sin? But I've realized it's impossible to ignore sin's effects. Evil is much more a part of me and my everyday than I ever wanted to admit.

So I had to examine myself in order to develop a strategy to let the good in me prevail.

First, I had to realize that making excuses for doing wrong goes back a long, long time. I'd developed a natural habit of making room for evil and even protecting it. I had to learn to watch out for this self-justifying, as I came to understand that ignorance really isn't bliss.

It surprised me to recognize how often I try to sidestep issues when I'm stuck. That's what I was doing in the checkout line at Home Depot. I've instinctively learned to justify myself in order to bring some sort of resolution. It helps me ignore that I might be doing something wrong. I try to tell myself I'm actually not responsible. I bite my lip and hope I've pacified the debate with my conscience.

If that doesn't work, I try to make light of it and laugh it off. I want to think it's no big deal, so I try to make it cute and innocent, when it really isn't.

This kind of self-imposed ignorance can never erase the real effects of sin. Just ask the people who trusted their accountants and now have lost everything. Or the child whose parent ignored all the signs of abuse and never confronted the perpetrator. In reality, the battle never starts with these extreme examples. It ends up there. Ignoring sin doesn't really work, because it eventually leads to worse things.

Evil in increased intensity is always trying to fly in just under the radar, and it will slip through every time if we aren't careful.

I've come to respect that sin starts small, as a tiny spark. That's the trap, because it's easier to ignore at this stage. For me, if I'm not watchful, if I think it's innocent, cute, or perfectly natural, the slow process of destruction builds. Evil is a patient adversary. It looks for the reliable long-term investments in my life.

Fortunately, I've always had a gut feeling about right and wrong. Even before I was specifically aware through the clarity that Jesus brought to the issue of evil, I was aware in a general sense. I think we all are to some degree. Then the teachings of Jesus helped me understand evil and its effects in a healthier and more productive way and to see that this wrestling is a good thing.

I think my moral dilemmas preserve my humanity, rather than letting me live by feelings and urges like an animal with no self-control. I just wish this wisdom wasn't buried so deeply in those tempting moments.

My first realization about sin was that I had to watch my tendency toward self-justification. Sin is actually part of my nature. I do it naturally. And I even protect my inclination toward it. To master it to any degree, I have to become extremely aware and examine myself whenever I am aware that I am justifying something.

I also became aware of a much deeper evil, one that was hidden for a long time by my self-justifying. It was like a backdoor I was tricked into leaving open so sin could come in whenever it wanted, like a secret but welcome guest.

It was time to close this door if I was ever going to win. I hated examining this bad habit. Once I was ready to face it, I had to ask myself what specific part of me it had affected. That was uncomfortable. I knew right away. It hit me like a ton of bricks. I was ashamed, and I knew changing would take even more work.

I had to go back and dig deep.

A Firefight

I remember it well. I remember the name of the movie. I even remember the brand of the VCR I played it on when no one was around.

Afterward I was sick to my stomach and ashamed. But I was also curious for more.

It was the same feeling my best friend had a few days later when I showed it to him. After a few minutes he said, "Okay, now turn it back on!" It fueled something inside. It was a dark flame. I could feel it then. And I still feel it now.

I was eleven years old, and that was the first adult movie I'd ever seen. I hesitate to share that detail of my life. It would be easier to write about other people. You know, "my friend" or "someone I once knew." But that would be insincere. It's a disgusting part of my life. I think it clearly tells the story of ugliness that's waiting for an opportunity to surface in all of us at any time. Not everyone's ugliness is the same, but there's something there in everyone. And that's why I tell it.

As a teenager, I was obsessed by pornography. No one who knew me then would know. Those with addictive habits are excellent at hiding them. Somehow, we're convinced there's nothing wrong with what we're doing, while at the same time we carry a sense of shame and try to hide our behavior. That should tell us something.

I know some people don't think what I was into is such a big deal, that it's all part of growing up—the whole "exploring and experimenting" thing. After all, it's natural.

I couldn't disagree more.

I found it consuming me emotionally and mentally. It caused me to develop an unhealthy image of women. Along with my parents' divorce, my mother not being around much, and feeling alienated in my own home, it served to foster that unhealthy habit and bad side of my nature.

And twenty-five years later, the effects still linger.

My past haunts me. Every day. Whether I'm going to the grocery story, watching a comedy, or swinging a hammer working on a project, I feel the bad Jason. He's waiting patiently to start the debate, fuel the urge, win over my mind, prompt an action, change my behavior, evolve into an unhealthy habit, and ruin the life I'm trying to build. These actions became part of who I am forever, and I fight the progression every day, because my evil side is an extremely effective strategist.

It's true I was young and foolish. I was also empty and looking to feel validated. I settled for feeling good, and it was a counterfeit. Like a parasite, these addictive and obsessive habits attached themselves to the foundation of the person I was still becoming, and they began eating away at me and destroying my humanity.

There's no question in my mind that my personality—who I actually am—has been shaped by this indulgence. To this day, I struggle with the same things I did as a youth, and I'm often ashamed at how weak I feel at times.

I am always seeking change and purity. I wish I could make this dark nature inside me go away. But I can't.

I realized that I could, however, build my strength against it by working on my strategy—and sticking with it.

For me, identifying the beginning of this was crucial to figuring out how to fight for my good side and win more often. I had to recognize when it all started to become so ugly for me. I had to know what door to close. But more than closing a door, I had to dig up the weeds at their roots. I couldn't just keep planting around them. It explained why the bad in me had become so much more difficult to tame.

Going back is never fun, but I had to figure out what my big failings stemmed from, why I was so weak. So to win more, I remember the past and what it's done to me. It keeps me even more aware of what to watch out for and stay away from.

Warning Shots

But that's still not enough. My strategy to be the good Jason only begins with being watchful of my justifying and more aware of sin's biggest foothold in my life. Beyond that, I also have to be aware of the times when I'm most vulnerable. The draw is so powerfully seductive that it can still pull me down even when my watchful eyes are on patrol. Sometimes those eyes get tired and close for a moment. I can easily give in when I'm caught a little off balance.

When my oldest son was very young, he was fascinated with vacuum cleaners. It was strange. He was never afraid of them like many toddlers. When he heard it being taken out of the utility closet, he would come running, calling its name. He couldn't say "vacuum" quite right, so he came racing around the corner hollering, *"Bapoo!"*

He wouldn't leave Bapoo's side. As my wife vacuumed, he stood next to it with his little hand on top of it, like it was his best friend.

When the time came to put it away, distress followed. He would lean on the closet door with his head down calling, "Bapoo, Bapoo!" as if he were saying, "Don't worry, old friend; I promise we'll be together again soon!"

But he wasn't particularly loyal. He was equally enamored with all vacuums. When we went shopping, he could spot them all the way across the store. He would motion, asking in his own way to go see his friends. It was so endearing.

Vacuum cleaners had a strange power over him. They seemed to cast a spell. He couldn't help himself. They would consume him and render him oblivious to anything else. They were his Achilles' heel, his kryptonite.

Although I'm not a toddler, I'm not much different—just more sophisticated.

As aware as I am of my tendency toward certain evils, they still manage to cast spells on me. I think it's true for all of us. When we're having a bad week, or we've been fighting at home, or something really awful happens and life is all-around suckie or stressful, it's the thing we think about doing to bring some comfort and inebriate us with good feelings. It could be ice cream, a drink, shopping, or something more serious. It simply offers an escape that normal life doesn't. In moderation and the right context, it might not even be a bad thing. But it can get bad.

I've noticed my bad side likes to focus on a normal appetite, one that's perfectly fine and natural, and distort it. Desires for food, sex, or something else become all consuming and unhealthy. Like the vacuums for my son, they temporarily mesmerize us and we make decisions we would not normally make. They try to get us to open the door just once. After all, once isn't so bad, and it will never happen again, right? Wrong. Don't be fooled.

In weaker moments, we're drawn to them like metal to a magnet or a moth to a flame. And make no mistake; it hurts like a flame. Your bad side gets you to give in and take the focus off what's happening, and the cycle's on.

Not only is evil patient—it's never satisfied until it has ruined everything.

So, I try to be especially alert when I may be weak. Otherwise, I start to change back into the bad Jason. He gets lonely. He's always awake, waiting for a moment to break out.

Basic Retraining

Jesus talked plainly and frequently about sins like lust, greed, anger, and deceit. And for a very real reason.

I know for me, whether I might classify certain wrongs as bigger or worse than others, they all affect my character. *Who I am* is actually changed by my bad choices, and they get in the way of *who I want to be.* That's what sin wants to do. It wants to destroy the person and his life. Evil, like misery, loves company; it loves chaos, disorder, and destruction.

For me, any degree of giving in will often leave me impatient, angry, depressed, self-centered, closed, and unforgiving. At first, I don't notice. But I know I've become less vigilant when I start asking myself questions like:

Why am I so touchy?

Why did they do that to me?

Why doesn't anyone appreciate me?

Why did I blow up over that?

Why don't I follow through with stuff?

Why do I always see the negative?

These questions are all about how *I* feel. They reveal that I've started turning into another person. I stop recognizing myself, as do those around me. My sin creates a wake that damages my relationships. It destroys opportunities and limits intimacy.

What to do? If being watchful and aware isn't enough—if sin can still hit and win when I'm down—what can I do?

To gain more strength against sin, I try to starve my particular appetite for it. As much as I try to watch and use self-control, the only way I win is to avoid the things that get me. When I'm having moments of weakness (we all know about those), I try to walk away and divert my focus.

I try to create a new, healthier way of getting through these times. Instead of giving in, I take a walk, call a friend, balance the bills, read a book, throw the ball around with the dog, or take the kids to the park. I try to starve the appetite before it becomes unhealthy, before it starves me of my strength to resist. And in the process, I protect my character and take another step toward becoming the person I want to be.

But beware: *Starving it won't make the appetite go away.* Evil's never gone. The strategy I've put together simply lessens its appeal and makes one stronger to stand against it.

Some battles aren't as ugly as others. I've also noticed the battles change and evolve with time, as I do. My appetites evolve, so I always try to remember that I'm just two to three decisions away from ruining what matters most to me.

A Civil War

Is this all too big of a trip to lay on myself? Am I beating myself up too much? Doesn't Jesus want me to ease up a little?

No way. There's even more I do to trick myself.

I've often told myself I'm not that bad, I'm basically a good person, I'm not as bad as so-and-so, and, after all, I've never murdered anyone. I've even said my problem is personal and doesn't affect anyone else. I try to rationalize it all and make it seem like no big deal, make it seem more civilized than it really is.

As much as I hate it, this is why I've had to learn to be comfortable calling this stuff "sin" and to realize I have a bad side. If I don't, I start treating these wrong things as "mistakes." And if something's only a mistake, I don't have to take full responsibility for it; I can convince myself, and maybe others, that it was just an accident, and I didn't mean to do it.

That's neither true, nor healthy.

If I don't take responsibility, I'll be less likely to apologize and try to repair the damage I've done, and I'll never change or grow as a person. Or as I heard it said one night while munching popcorn and sipping a Coke and watching Jack Bauer in *24,* "Part of getting a second chance is taking responsibility for the mess you made in the first place." Too bad it was a writer for a fictional character in a made-up story that had that insight.

Whether we call them sins, mistakes, mess-ups, or whatever, our selfish, parasitic habits are real, and they lay down a subtle path of destruction. For me, calling sin merely a "mistake" is always the precursor for a bigger failing—when there's no doubt how bad it is.

So, I try not to kid myself. It's *not* an accident when I lie to a friend. There's no "oops" when I take what doesn't belong to me. It's not innocent. It's sin, and it's wrong.

Recon

Every so often, I make an effort to be deeply reflective and cathartic. It works only if it's peppered with humility and sober thinking. I take stock of the recent past and assess my personal character and progress. The questions usually grow deeper, and I resist the temptation to be sidetracked with something like checking email or answering a phone call. These are all about how what I do affects others.

I start by asking myself:

Have I been honest with others?

Have I been fair in my dealings?

Have I been unselfish most of the time?

Have I put others first most of the time?

Have I shut my big mouth most of the time, and not said whatever comes to mind?

Have I resisted the urge to get the last word?

Have I exercised self-control?

Have I focused on the positive?

Have I said kind things to my wife?

Have I encouraged my kids?

Have I spent our money wisely?

It's a difficult process, but helpful. It's the only way to measure the state of my affairs and character.

I find that I still seem to do a lot of damage. That's why I set personal goals and assess them. That plainly helps, and I hope the result is that I will bring more good than evil into my immediate surroundings and this world. That's my real goal. It may be small, but it's something to build from.

We all have appetites to manage and two sides to control. Our bad sides will never go away, but the more we nurture our good sides, the easier it gets.

It's a lot like the results of all the hard work I did on our first house. It took a lot of labor and constant attention. It wasn't easy, but it was totally worth it. In the end, the house we built was beautiful. As we build and remodel ourselves into new and better people, the shadowy, seductive voices can be muffled to faint whispers. The threatening flame can flicker down to a smoldering ember. And the beautiful days can continue.

This is the challenge. Whether we like it or not, we're going to live from one of those two sides, the good or the bad. I say let it be the better one. Let's create a "new you."

Once you've made that decision, then something can happen: *You can change.* This is how you know your strategies are working. You become the better person you want to be.

The Peacemaker

But even with all that, there's still guilt to deal with. I'm aware of my inability to do the right thing all the time, even though that's my deepest desire.

The fact is, as much as I manage to change, I'll never achieve perfection. As successful as I may become in living from my good side, I'll never be good enough. As much as I starve my appetite for doing bad, I will still indulge it. And since I can't accomplish a consistent, flawless victory over my sin, the guilt remains. As a result, the evil I do, though I don't wish to do it, makes me feel distant from God. How do I restore the connection? How do I take away the sense of guilt, heal the relationship, and bridge the gap?

I've learned to ask for forgiveness. That's the only remedy.

Forgiveness is why Jesus came to earth. It's what makes him so popular. Many people resist the thought that they need forgiveness in regard to their standing with God. That's fine; I'm not trying to convince people they're bad. I'm just telling you that I am, and what I do about it, because unresolved guilt seems to turn my heart bitter and angry.

On the night before Jesus was put to death, he gathered his followers one last time. He knew what was coming, so he asked them to prepare a last meal together. It was the Last Supper, and Leonardo DaVinci painted his rendition of it. I think the reality of that occasion was much more somber and dark than the painting captures. The air was probably heavy with anxiety and dread. I love that perspective even more than what the painting conveys. It's not as pretty or aesthetically pleasing — but something beautiful was about to happen.

My wife has given birth three times, all by C-section. I'm not comparing this to what Jesus endured — being beaten and crucified, but the pain she went through in the process was horrible. It's by far the most brutal experience I've ever witnessed. The sounds and smells in the operating room and the clinical, detached demeanor of the doctors and nurses made it even worse. Though I'm six-foot-two and well over two hundred pounds, I was on the verge of passing out on the operating room floor every time one of our children was born.

And the recoveries were vicious for her. At least when it was all over and the wounds were healed, we had the new objects of our love, our babies. In the end, after all the pain, there was beauty.

Jesus knew that his gruesome death would usher in something new God was doing. The night before, as his meal with them was ending, he wanted to comfort his disciples with a vision of what was coming, though they didn't quite get it. He described the event at hand and assured them it was necessary.

You know what happened next. His horrible suffering came. But afterward, there was, and is, beauty.

And it was all to undo the effects of sin. If humanity could comprehend this and ask for forgiveness, God would grant it—total and complete.

In the spirit of what Jesus did, I acknowledge my sin, and the guilt is erased. Long ago, I made a decision that no matter what wrong I did or how ashamed I felt, I would face God. I wouldn't let my failings keep me away. And each time, I'm reunited with my Creator.

That's not to say I'm careless in what I do, knowing I'll be forgiven anyway. Many Christians do that. I've done it. But it's immature to presume on the grace of God like that.

Visualizing the sadness Jesus must have felt in that upper room sobers me.

When I fall short and acknowledge my limitations, God is faithful to restore the relationship. He forgives me and we move on. In fact, he remembers the incident no more.

Winning the Battle

I hate bringing up this chapter's topic. Who the heck wants to talk about sin? I hate sin more than ever. But if I don't tackle it personally, I'll never try to change the man I am into the vision of the man I want to become.

About Home Depot—I guess I left it hanging. There I was at the checkout counter, wrestling with myself. I reluctantly asked the cashier if she was sure that was the correct amount. We checked my receipt against the items on my cart. Sure enough, she had made a mistake. A big mistake. She thanked me, but it didn't seem heartfelt. I thought she could at least call the manager over so I would be rewarded with an even bigger discount. You know, customer appreciation. Nope. Nobody really cared.

It was anticlimactic. But in the end, it turned into one of the rare times I actually did the right thing. And it was a good day.

We all have good days and bad ones. The good ones fuel us and make us stronger. They're beautiful days. And with a strategy in mind for dealing with my sin, and with forgiveness at heart, I look forward to lots more of them.

#5 Rules

Everybody's heard it: you can choose your friends, you can choose your enemies, but you can't choose your family.

If I *could* choose, I think my father would be a cross between Arnold Schwarzenegger, Winston Churchill, and Donald Trump. Then I'd have all the makings of strength, character, and drive—a great formula for success and happiness, if you ask me. My mother would be a combination of Mother Teresa, Joan of Arc, and Audrey Hepburn. This would add the much-needed balance of sacrifice, devotion, and grace to my personality.

But the mix of inherited personalities most of us are born with seems to be lighter on success formulas and heavier on, well, baggage.

It was Thanksgiving week, and we had some family visiting. It's a funny thing when relatives visit. You're happy to see them. And you're happy to see them go. Anyway, mine flew in at the beginning of the week, and by Thanksgiving, the tension was noticeable. At least mine was.

Thanksgiving itself had the makings of a good day. There would be huge amounts of tasty food from morning till night. Who isn't comforted by that prospect? Everything started right with coffee and cinnamon rolls. By ten a.m., we were hitting the drinks (Coke for me, Sprite for my kids and wife, wine for the visiting relatives). We were chasing it down with chips-n-dip, shrimp cocktail, and half a dozen other appetizers. Plus, we were sampling the food we were cooking for dinner.

My boys joined right in. They went around the house eating. And eating. And eating. Like a fat guy at a buffet (like me). But I know my boys. They were 7 months and two and a half at the time, and they hadn't figured out how to gauge their fullness. Eventually, I told them to stop eating until dinner.

My relatives, however, didn't think that was fair. After all, we kept sampling everything; were the kids just supposed to watch?

Yes!

I reminded my family members, since they'd apparently forgotten what it was like to parent young children, that since kids are not adults, they aren't yet entitled to fair treatment in every arena of life like the Bill of Rights promises. I also reminded them who the parent was.

I thought my speech worked, but they managed to sneak snacks to the kids when my wife and I weren't looking. I caught them a few times and reprimanded them, but they wouldn't listen. My impatience kicked in. My relatives were interfering.

The day went on, and the aromas were glorious—turkey in the

oven, stuffing, sweet potatoes, mashed potatoes, simmering gravy. Finally, it was time for dinner. We all sat down, the food was passed around, and our plates were filled. Forks were drawn, and it was time to dig in.

Just as we were all about to take that first mouth-watering bite, there was a loud, guttural roar, something universal in every culture and language: *HOOWRUULAAW!* The sound of someone throwing up.

Right there at the Thanksgiving table, my oldest boy barfed. Out of him came chips, soda, chocolate milk, shrimp, M&Ms, dip, more chips, more shrimp, Cheetos—all half-digested, all out there for everyone to see and smell. The concoction overflowed his plate, cascaded down the table's edge, splashed into his lap, ran down his legs, and puddled on the floor beneath him.

I was pissed. A once-a-year event—one you look forward to all year—was ruined.

I wasn't mad at my son. I was mad because a rule was ignored. Just one rule. A rule for a reason. A rule with a benefit. And ignoring it had harvested the result I knew it would. It wasn't fair to my son or to us.

That rule had a purpose. It wasn't mindless.

Rebel Just Because

I've concluded there are two types of people in this world. There are the goody-two-shoes who like rules and take great pride in creating and obeying them. And there are the other people. The ones who like to rebel. The ones who never saw a rule, standard, or principle they didn't salivate to defy. They like breaking rules.

I hate rules. Like most people (and my visiting relatives at Thanksgiving), I decide when I want to follow them. I love that autonomy. Most of us do. We're not going to let anyone or anything tell us what to do or how to do it.

I tend to push against rules because I don't always see their benefits in the moment. But even if I could, it probably wouldn't matter. I want to do what I want to do when I want to do it.

And if just one rule gets me edgy, what about dozens?

It didn't take long before I got the impression Christianity was filled with rules. Jesus I found compelling, but I started to wonder why someone would ever want to be a Christian with all those rules that seemed to go with the territory.

I soon began to hate the rules and, as a result, to hate Christianity. The rules made me think God didn't want me to have any fun. Like he was some sour old man yelling at the neighborhood kids, "Keep it down out there *or else!*" But we all want to have fun; it makes life worth living. If we can't enjoy it, what's the point to life?

It seemed impossible to keep up with all the rules, not to mention I hated a lot of them. I didn't know to what degree Christians were making them up. At first, I assumed they were probably in the Bible. So, they had to be kept, right? And God was going to make me give up everything I liked if I kept following him. That was frustrating and overwhelming. I liked my fun, and rules brought an air of legalism that sapped the life and vitality out of anything good. Legalism does that.

But, like most people I've talked to about these rules, I wasn't actually that familiar with them. So, I determined to discover more about the rules I'd started to hate so much.

I can't keep track of all the rules I've been told to keep over the years, so I'll just hit on the most common ones—like no smoking, drinking, cussing, premarital sex, clubbing, or dancing.

But wait, there's more! If one decides to *really* get serious about following God, there's another set of rules for the "truly religious"—like no listening to "secular" music (music that isn't "Christian"), no watching R-rated movies, no dating, no tattoos, no body piercings.

As far as I can tell, these rules are meant to address character issues. They call into question the things that influence you, what you take in, and how it all affects who you are. They also call into question what you choose to do, which is seen as a representation of who you are.

As I explored the rules, I put them into categories. The first overall category is the one relating to entertainment activities—music, movies, and dancing, in particular. I break these rules a lot.

Backyard BBQ

Early on, some Christians told me that "anything not of God is of the devil," and that I had to get rid of all my "secular" music tapes and albums. So I did, in a big ball of flames. Burning them was the only right thing to do, they said; if I sold them or gave them away, I'd only be causing other people to be influenced by devil music.

Looking back, I'm mad about that. I had some good albums and some rare, colored vinyl. But at the time, I trusted what these Christians were telling me, and I forced myself to listen to only "Christian" music.

But the rule started to break down in my mind. I wondered: *What really is Christian music?*

Is it hymns? Boring! On my way home from work in traffic on a Friday afternoon, I'm not rocking out to hymns with organ music and harps, thank you very much. It's just not happening.

Or does "Christian" music mean it's supposed to be about and represent Jesus? If so, I assume it would have a certain level of excellence. That seems reasonable. Unfortunately, I've listened to a lot of Christian music, and much of it just isn't that good or original. Actually, it sucks. Why should I force myself to listen to something I don't like?

In fairness, Christians do make some of my favorite music. It's called *Christmas* music. But the rest of the year, the no-secular-music rule is hard to keep. To get me through traffic, mowing the lawn, or a creative lull, I listen to artists like U2, the Clash, the Beatles, Johnny Cash, Metallica, Depeche Mode, New Order, Coldplay, Sarah McLachlan, Madness, Frank Sinatra, Sade, Midnight Oil, Bob Marley, John Mayer, Radiohead, Gorilla Biscuits, The Cro-Mags, Sunny Day Real Estate, the Police, Norah Jones, the Cure, James Brown, Beastie Boys, Fugazi, Run DMC, Sex Pistols, Helmet, Slayer, and Ella Fitzgerald.

From my experience, there's nothing in the Bible mandating that we listen exclusively to music that's allegedly "Christian." To arrive at this rule, I think Christians stretch certain Bible passages, which to me means that this isn't really a rule at all. It's somebody's suggested guideline, which may or may not be beneficial.

Besides, where does this Christian-secular distinction end? Does the car I drive have to be "Christian"? And the clothes I wear?

So what's worse: going around insisting on these rules and coming off as some militant freak or just letting people listen to the music they like?

I get how this type of rule is geared toward youth, who are really influenced by pop culture. And as a parent, I'll gauge somewhat what my kids listen to. But in a gray area like this, I just don't want to give them some legalistic trip that messes up how they view God. And once they're of age, I couldn't care less what they listen to. Secular or Christian, a good song is a good song.

Food for Thought

I absolutely love movies. I always have. It's how I refuel on days off. I actually feel my stress release as I watch some of my favorites. I can't tell you how many times I've seen *Alien, Aliens, Gladiator, Braveheart, The Matrix, Last of the Mohicans, Highlander, We Were Soldiers, Gangs of New York, Crash, Blade Runner, Terminator, Return of the Living Dead, Dawn of the Dead, Saw, Conan the Barbarian, The Patriot, Black Hawk Down, Ronin,* and *The Last Samurai.* But all these are rated R.

Another rule broken.

In principle, this rule is similar to the music rule. But there are very few officially "Christian" movies, and those that are tend to be so bad they aren't really acknowledged. So this rule is modified. As I found out early on, I'm not supposed to watch movies rated R. PG-13 is okay, PG is better, and G is the best.

That rule *never* worked for me. Sometimes I just want something raw and emotional. I want to see a story with actual conflict and real-istic resolution, because that's how life is. Plus, there are plenty of R-rated movies that aren't as bad as some PG-13s I've seen.

Again, in my understanding, there's really no passage in the

Bible that spells out anything like this. Of course, unlike music, there was never anything like a movie around when the Bible was written, so this rule is a reach by its very nature.

I was told that in the Bible the apostle Paul says to think on things that are pure, good, holy, and respectable,[3] and that R-rated movies don't have a lot of that in them. I get that, but I also like good movies that tell good stories about things in real life. Good stories in which a character evolves can be somewhat virtuous. Either way, it's entertainment to me. I'm not watching a movie to imitate it or learn from it. I realize it's not real.

And what about a movie like R-rated *Schindler's List?* It tells the story of the plight of the Jews in World War II in a way that needs to be told.

To some degree, I can see the benefit of this rule. Based on my past, I'm not comfortable watching sex scenes and nudity. It conjures old memories. So I suppose there are limits that each individual has to consider when approaching the content of a movie. But again, that's more of a guideline and not quite a rule.

Can someone like the R-rated movie *Saving Private Ryan* and still follow Jesus with all his heart? Why not? Besides, the highest grossing R-rated movie of all time was *The Passion of the Christ.* Now there's some irony.

Simmer Down

Then there's the rule against dancing and a related one against clubbing.

I became a Christian in high school, so the no-dancing rule came into play for me when senior prom was approaching. Not that I was dying to dance, or even can dance, but was I allowed to?

There's nothing like this rule in the Bible. Not even close. In fact, there's quite a bit of dancing in the Bible and it's normally a good thing. For example, King David danced because he was excited about how much God loved him.[4]

So, I decided to break the rule and dance at my prom. It was a scary sight, as I sported the white man's overbite in every ungraceful move. But it was a fun time. We all goofed off.

After high school, I went to clubs a little. It was usually to be the designated driver for my cousin. Later I stopped, though not because I thought it was specifically wrong. Clubs always had an abundance of girls and booze, and every time I went, I ended up doing things I shouldn't and didn't want to do. But the next time my cousin asked me to go, I'd convince myself I'd be stronger this time. I never was, so I stopped, and no clubbing became a personal rule for me, since I was trying to resist old habits. Isn't it amazing how many opportunities to do something arise when you're trying *not* to do it?

So can Christians dance or go to clubs? I guess some can and some can't. For me, it became a moral decision for reasons unrelated to dancing or clubbing itself. What it led to was the problem. Dancing itself isn't wrong—though maybe those Christians who have no rhythm can spare us their gyrations.

Smoked Turkey

A second category of the rules I heard from Christians had to do with health issues.

From what I was told, smoking is a sin—it's *really* wrong. Personally, I find it disgusting, so I never had a problem with this rule. But I still wanted to find out the validity of it.

Again, I found no rule against it in the Bible. It's not that smoking wasn't around back then; it's just not mentioned. So this rule, too, is something someone made up—a good guideline at best, not a rule to base your spirituality on.

The reasons given for this rule are that it's bad for you, you're supposed to take care of the body God gave you, and you'll "reap what you sow." That last thought—the idea that there are negative and positive consequences to certain actions—*is* throughout the Bible.[5] If you sow to your unhealthy habits, you'll reap the effects.

What do you "reap" when you smoke? Well, there's the odor on your clothes, in your hair, on your breath, in your apartment, and in your car. Also, your kids may be breathing in unhealthy secondhand smoke. And if you take a lot of smoke breaks at work, you may be less productive. There's also that nasty old cancer thing. A neighbor of mine was just diagnosed with terminal lung cancer. He's sixty-seven and quit smoking many years ago, but it caught up with him.

Of course, the reap-what-you-sow principle can get just as heavy when you bring it to the logical conclusion in lots of other areas. It can be applied as much to the five tacos I just ate as it can to smoking. Smoking's easier to single out because it's becoming more socially unacceptable.

But smoke up if that's what you want, if you can live with the consequences. And if you enjoy it, toke. I toked a little socially as a young teenager, but eventually realized my desire to be cool wasn't as great as my desire not to be sick.

Liquid Diet

I was also told that true Christians don't drink. This one was confusing. Practically everybody in the Bible drank; there were no refrigerators back then, and fermented drinks kept well, so that's mostly what people drank. Often, water wasn't safe to drink, so this was the only solution.

But that doesn't deter some committed keepers of this rule. They claim that the booze back in Bible times was so watered-down it was really like grape juice. That's a real stretch. For one thing, watered down grape juice eventually spoils when it's not refrigerated. I have kids, so I know. Wine back then had to be well fermented (i.e., *strong*) in order to keep.

So there's no real rule against drinking. Again, just be smart about it. The Bible *does* warn about getting drunk. It encourages us to behave decently and not get drunk and do crazy things because of drinking.[6] And it says the people who get drunk often become poor through their lack of judgment.[7]

This is the reaping-and-sowing principle again, and it's hard to argue with. Most people have friends who prove this to be true. Inevitably, when people drink too much, they end up doing things they wouldn't normally do if they had all their senses about them, and they later regret those things.

I take what the Bible says as a warning to be aware of your limits and not get drunk. Otherwise, you might talk back to a boss at an after-hours meeting. You might have a violent outbreak and get in a fight. You could cheat on someone you love.

Plus, there are long-term health issues like liver disease. Or you can lose your driving privileges, or worse, kill someone while driving.

One of my clients lost her teenage daughter from that. The daughter was in a car with three friends when they were hit and instantly killed by a drunk driver. I'm sure that guy thought he was under control, but his lack of judgment brought tragic consequences.

Personally, I have nothing against drinking, except that I find the taste of alcohol revolting. Plus, it hasn't ever added anything beneficial to my life. I think everyone has relatives who will communicate about real issues only after a few drinks, and afterward they don't remember the conversations. Cycles continue, apologies lose their meaning, promises are left unfulfilled, and the relationships don't get any better. So I guess I'd much rather have a Coke and a smile.

But feel free to slam back a forty in my memory when I die, if that suits your taste.

I suppose rules like no smoking and no drinking are meant to call into question our health habits and behaviors. I respect that. If I have a problem with managing my cravings and indulgences, I need to work on my self-control. If I can't be disciplined, then perhaps I'm not maturing as a whole. I understand that perspective, but it's not always the case.

Who's to say a cigarette is any worse than a bag of M&M's? My wife has that addiction, but it doesn't bother me much. Who's to say drinking too many beers is any worse than spending yourself deeply into debt? Both can have lasting, unintended consequences that affect many.

In all honesty, these are gray areas. Again, each person has to decide for himself or herself and weigh the consequences.

Comfort Food

I put the next group of rules in the category of relationships. A big one here is that some Christians say you're not supposed to date; instead, you should "court."

The thinking, as I understand it, is that you shouldn't have a romantic relationship with anyone you don't see as marriage material. Otherwise, it will end painfully for both people. It will be emotionally messy and hurtful. I understand that. Often we're left feeling like we never want to do this again.

That's how I felt when Stephanie dumped me in seventh grade. I've never fully recovered from that rejection. She was gorgeous. (I also have no idea why she ever said yes to dating me, especially since she was in eighth grade.) Pizza and ice cream helped to heal my broken heart.

I think the no-dating idea really takes to task the dating-for-sport approach that we learn from a young age. It tries to give more importance to creating and pursing relationships other than for recreation. Honestly, this is probably a good thing, since our culture is so highly sexualized.

If you decide you shouldn't date unless you can see yourself eventually marrying that person, then you'll probably want to first get to know someone really well. When you court you decide to just be friends and hang out in groups. There's less risk of pain and hurt. That's good, but it still pretty much sounds like dating to me. I think it's just semantics.

To me, this rule is tricky. I know every girl I ever dated wasn't necessarily the one I thought I'd marry, not even the woman who eventually became my wife. Sure, marriage was always a goal for me, but I always felt I first had to get to know someone better before thinking about that. How am I supposed to learn about who someone is as a person if we're always in big groups and casually distant environments? This is where it gets confusing for me. For this relational discovery to happen, it needed a dating type of setting.

And let's be honest. If a girl says she wants to "just be friends," a guy's doomed. There won't be a romantic connection, and she doesn't really care about getting to know him. Unless it will help get her homework done or her car washed.

And if a guy says he wants to "just be friends," he's either not attracted to the girl, or he's lying. That's what I said to Lisa (now my wife) when we met. I was full on lying. I thought she was a hottie.

It's not very spiritual to admit it, but guys aren't interested in being friends with girls unless they find the girls unattractive. That's the cold, hard truth. Guys can't be friends with girls. (See *When Harry Met Sally* for more on this, if you watch R-rated movies.)

So, if a guy finds a girl attractive *and* says he just wants to be friends, it's because he's actually looking for an opportunity. It can also mean he thinks the girl is way out of his league and so he wants to get in good with her and eventually woo her into a romantic connection.

A guy will then employ all his wiles and everything he can think of to win her over: casually remembering her birthday, her mom's birthday, and her best friend's birthday; opening doors for her; writing her poems and notes; giving her a music mix she likes that he "just happened" to be listening to; seeing romantic comedies and even saying afterward how much he just loved it (this highlights his sensitive side); joining a yoga class; talking to her on the phone at length and text-messaging extensively (this highlights his ability and willingness to communicate); and enthusiastically offering to take care of her cat or toy poodle. All this is to make her fall in love with him.

But these ploys don't work in the end. Since this isn't really who he is, she'll end up figuring it out. Girls always do.

Free Samples

I think the no-dating rule exists because of some of the unhealthy consequences dating often leads to. Dating can bring a deep-level intimacy that should be reserved for someone you're in a committed relationship with, someone you're married to. Dating often leads to sex.

So the no-dating rule for many is really rooted in another rule, one that's actually from the Bible: we're not supposed to have sex with anyone other than our spouses. In this context, Christians have some valuable insight into the whole relationship thing.

The Bible's clear on this one. There's no arguing here. This rule is one of the Ten Commandments. Jesus reinforced this rule in his teachings.[8] He also took it to a higher level and said if we even look at someone else and think about having sex, it's as bad as gettin' it on with her.[9] Ouch! I'd rather not dwell on that.

The no-premarital-sex rule can be difficult because it deals with a natural desire. One that isn't bad. One that God put there. But he also pointed out a context for that desire. So, I can't explain away this rule, though it's tempting to try, since it feels so good to break.

I think that's why so many people try to outthink God on this one. They say (I've said it too) that this rule's outdated. They don't want to let something as wonderful as their love be limited or defined by anybody's old rule. Sound familiar? A guy will often say something like that as he tries to get a girl to break the rule. Then he'll finish with, "If you really love me, you will…"

Let's be honest: some people just want to "get busy" and have sex. There's nothing wrong with that in its proper context, which is one of the reasons I got married.

But God had a reason behind making this rule. It's interesting how many relationships fall apart when they ignore it. If breaking this rule were so right, wouldn't the math back that up? But it doesn't. People who have sex and aren't married usually don't stay together. And those who do get married have higher divorce rates than those who don't have sex before marriage. They're also at higher risk for disease, depression, addiction, and many other health issues.

I'm not trying to elevate myself. I "did it." And I hate the residual memories that pop up at the strangest times for no reason at all. I'm not proud of it. It's as if I impulsively gave a piece of myself away to someone. More to the point, in the heat of a moment, I took a part of someone that didn't belong to me. It belonged to the man who would marry her, who would make and maintain a lifelong commitment.

I've always wanted to be good in this area. I even told my wife when we were still dating, "I'll never try anything." That was a load of crap. I wish I would have respected her more and not been such a stupid, typical guy. So what if everyone else does it? *She deserved better.* I know our marriage has suffered and been difficult at times because I undermined her trust in me. I thought I knew more than God in these instances, and it wasn't so smart.

Looking back, I'm sorry for breaking that promise I made to her. And I know what I should have done. I should never have promised her anything. *Just kidding!* What I should have done is kept my word and never tried anything.

I've heard all the arguments against this rule. Especially this one: "You have to find out if you're sexually compatible with a person." But this kind of impulsive, rash, impetuous, instinctive, primal, emotional basis for a relationship is in truth *not* compatible with any long-term commitment.

True compatibility is built on respect and trust. True chemistry — the lasting bond that sustains a relationship, making it healthier — is also built on trust and respect. It's fostered by a long-term commitment that builds and strengthens with more time and investment. An old woman once told a girlfriend of mine, "If you're giving away the milk, why should a guy buy the cow?" Take it from a guy; it's true.

All this may fly in the face of pop psychology and social trends, but relationships truly stop working when one participant *chooses* to stop being compatible. He allows a breakdown in the foundational elements of trust and respect. She *chooses* to stop loving. That's why people aren't compatible. And the math backs me up on that.

Saying this, I can hear the groans and see the eyes rolling. *He's so over-simplifying this!* But think about a mystery that's been going on for centuries: *People choose to love a person they don't even know.* These people are called *expectant parents.* Through an amazing phenomenon, they love their unborn child more than they can describe, often more than they've ever loved anyone. It happens before they ever meet this little individual, *before* ever finding out if they have compatible personalities or good chemistry, and before that person has any chance to earn or deserve their love. They've already *chosen* to love that little person.

Love is clearly a choice, and if we choose to stop loving someone, that's when we start becoming incompatible and the chemistry disappears.

So hate this rule all you want. Break it all you want. But there will be consequences. Sometimes physical, but always emotional. It's more likely you will *not* be compatible with the person you break this rule with in your effort to be more compatible.

Icing on the Cake

The next rules I put in the category of character and reputation. Not because keeping or breaking these rules necessarily says anything about that, but because that's often the perception.

First, Christians supposedly aren't allowed to get tattoos or piercings.

I have three tattoos. I got them after I became a Christian. I knew the rule, but I broke it anyway. I just wanted them bad. After that, I stopped, because I found out they were really addicting. I'm hard-pressed to meet anyone who's ever been satisfied with just one. But I stopped because I didn't want to turn into a freak show.

Don't get me wrong; I don't have a problem with lots of tats. I wish I had sleeves of tattoos. They look so rough and gritty. I love it, especially when it's just black ink. It looks so crisp traveling across the skin like a painted canvas. Can you tell I still want more? But they're expensive, they hurt really bad, I like being gainfully employed, and now I have kids.

Even though my tattoos don't bother me and I don't regret them *yet,* I know they bring consequences. I've often been treated like a criminal because I have tattoos. I have to cover them up in certain settings. And I have a sense of oncoming trouble because my young children have tried to rub them off while telling me not to write on myself.

When I got mine, I knew that the Bible actually said not to get tattoos.[10] But this rule made even less sense to me as I read the context of it, which also says not to wear clothes made from two different fabrics, not to cut the edges of your hair or shave the edges of your beards, and some other strange regulations that Christians today don't honor.

I have even recently reached a new plateau concerning tattoos. Two people contacted me to say they got tattoos of lyrics I wrote in tribute to the band I used to be in. The phrases were "I surrender all, all I am I give," and "Only love can fill the void." It's an honor. Not too many people can make such a boast. So you know I love those tats.

I've also had around nine piercings over the years, both before and after I started following Jesus. Most I did myself or had friends do with safety pins. But my earrings came out when I met my future wife, Lisa. She hated them. So, of course, I didn't like them anymore either (though at the time we were "just friends").

Every so often, I ask her if I can wear them again. Right now, she's telling me I can—if I lose forty pounds first. Not likely.

The Bible mentions many men and women that wore earrings and nose rings. For example, people gave them as gifts to God to help build their temple.[11] In a story God told, a nose ring and earrings were even described as beautiful ornaments he himself provided.[12]

And whenever earrings or nose rings show up in the Bible, there's no mention of a moral implication that I can find.

No one seems to have a problem with a woman having earrings. They mainly take issue when a guy does it, or when someone gets piercings in unconventional areas. The Bible doesn't mention piercings in these other areas. But I see no difference between a pierced nipple, or a pieced whatever, and a pierced ear or nose.

Again, I think Christians that promote these rules are just focusing on something they don't like or that makes them uncomfortable. It's pretty much a matter of taste—and pain tolerance, frankly. Nothing theological.

Salt & Peppered

Then there's the whole d#*n cussing thing. The Bible has plenty to say about our language. We're told to avoid corrupting or unwholesome talk and to only speak appropriate words that have a positive, helpful effect on other people.[13] We're also told that dirty, foolish talk and crude jokes are out of bounds.[14] And in one place we're challenged to ask ourselves how we can bless God in one breath, then curse someone in the next.[15]

So, I can see the connection.

I can't lie though. I cuss every once in a while. Usually it erupts from inside me when I smash my thumb with a hammer or my old truck breaks down. I'm not proud of it. I think it makes me sound pretty much like an idiot. And that's not who I want to be.

I know people who cuss like truckers, and it doesn't bother me one bit. But I'm of the opinion that peppering my own speech with these colorful phrases doesn't add anything to my life. It makes me sound silly and probably gives others the wrong impression.

I learned this firsthand.

Remember that Thanksgiving when my relatives were visiting? They left the following Sunday. That night we were putting my son to bed when he glared at my wife and said, "You a b*#ch." That was interesting. Now I know what you're thinking. I *promise,* we don't talk like that at home. I swear! It isn't, and wasn't, part of our vocabulary, especially in front of our kids. So, of course, we had our theories about where he picked up that magnificent word.

To their credit, I never heard my relatives use such words in front of our kids. But then again, I wasn't with them every second of every day during their visit. (They're still mad that I suspect them.)

It became a real problem when my son kept calling his mom that. Then he said it to the babysitter. Then he used it on his Sunday school teacher. This was a little awkward, considering I worked at the church.

It was an interesting situation to work through. Mainly, it misrepresented who we were. And it wasn't who we were trying to raise our kids to be.

For me, being a dad and a businessman, not cussing is a good idea. But I don't think any less of someone who cusses. I admit that there are times in life when it seems like nothing but a cussword will do. But that's not part of my regular speech.

The Secret Ingredient

In practice, I don't think any of the rules we've looked at have a bearing on a person's standing with God. Over the years, I've met several people who didn't listen to secular music, or watch R-rated movies, or dance, or cuss, or drink, and who were virgins when they got married—and they were complete jerks. They might have appeared close to God on the outside, but they misrepresented him in their character.

With regard to rules, right or wrong, every decision has consequences. Often, there's a price to pay for our choices. In that context, I understand the validity of most of these rules. They may even make one healthier and happier.

But they're not strict tenants of the Christian faith. And where the Bible is silent on certain issues, it's generally best for us to be silent as well. Some may choose to build their personal application of the Christian faith on these rules—and that might be wise and beneficial—but I don't necessarily assume it makes anyone less of a Christian if he doesn't observe them. God only knows.

So perhaps some rules have their place. If I look past the legalism and religiosity, I can see the rules are meant to keep people on track in their desire to follow God, to foster their devotion to him, and even to help them live healthier lives. But rules themselves don't necessarily make people more devoted or spiritually mature. They can be a catalyst for that if we have the right motivation. But without that, they can also choke out devotion. Rather than a representation of love and respect for God, they become a substitute for it, as rituals replace authentic relationships.

That's what Jesus often challenged the religious leaders on. He spoke about this a lot. He said the religious people had lost perspective on why God even gave rules. It became routine for them, having no real connection with God as their loving father.

In my marriage, I've found that certain practices we have—our date nights, gifts, my phone calls from work during the day—can become legalistic if I do them out of obligation alone. There's no real passion, and the relationship suffers. I think this can be true of any relationship, especially with God.

That's the real lesson about rules to me. If by applying and observing the rules, I'm drawn closer to the object of my love, or my love increases, then they're good. But if by keeping the rules I'm more impressed with myself, they fail, and they're wrong.

The Main Course

Although I hate them, clearly, rules can be a good thing.

After all, let's consider the real old-school rules—the Ten Commandments. You know, the ones God gave to Moses on the mountain. I can't ignore those. You've probably heard or read them. Most people think they're a good guide, regardless of their personal beliefs. I've met people who think they're good for keeping them and that they're on their way to heaven as a result.

Here they are, as paraphrased and understood by me:

Don't follow other gods. (Don't put possessions, pursuits, or passions before God.)

Don't worship created things or objects. (Don't put your faith or hope in a cross, statue, a "fish" sticker, a flag, some other symbol, or even nature.)

Don't take God's name or reputation lightly. (Don't cuss using God's name or his son's name, and don't say things like "I swear, as God is my witness.")

Don't work seven days a week. (You just can't go, go, go and do, do, do.)

Don't disrespect your parents.

Don't murder.

Don't have sex with anyone but your spouse.

Don't steal.

Don't lie.

Don't desire something you can't or shouldn't have. (Don't be consumed with thoughts of things that don't belong to you.)

So, those are the rules.

I'm old enough now to understand some of them. Not because I totally agree philosophically, but because I've learned their value the hard way, through the high-priced tuition my experiences have exacted.

I've actually honored each of these rules at different points in my life, but I still break quite a few of them. Breaking them eventually becomes habitual. It seems to run in cycles. I just can't help it. So, if I'll inevitably break some of these rules (either by omission or obstinance or both), how can I ever hope to maintain a connection with my Creator?

That's what drove me to examine all ten to make more sense of them.

Let's take a closer look at them, in a different light. I want to paraphrase the Ten Commandments again, but this time I want to capture what I feel is their true meaning. With a little poetic license, I want to communicate what I think God's really saying here. I've turned these ten into *do's* rather than don'ts:

Love God, and put him first. (Give him priority.)

Worship God. (Do whatever it takes to keep close to him, and let your relationship with him be the most valuable thing in your life.)

Say good things about God and his character.

Take a regular break from work. (Take a day off, rest, and be thankful for what you have.)

Respect your parents.

Respect others, and put them first whenever you can.

Be faithful to your spouse.

Be generous.

Be honest.

Strive to be content. (Appreciate what you have.)

Rules can be do's just as easily as don'ts. And there are benefits to most rules if I look at them that way. They can deepen devotion and strengthen relationships. They don't necessarily take away fun. Instead, they establish helpful boundaries. They protect us, keep us safe, promote healthy relationships, and even keep us alive.

I still hate rules, but I don't want to be the kind of person who gets excited about breaking them. It's just not cute to be well into your thirties, forties, or fifties and still whining like a rebellious teenager, "Stop telling me what to do!"

I'm not trying to tell you what to do or how to live. I'm not trying to interfere. But if you hate rules, ask yourself why.

I believe God wants us to have fun. Jesus even said he came to give us rich and exciting lives.[16] That doesn't sound boring.

So, do you like tattoos? Get one. Get a few dozen. Whatever. Do you like piercings? Go for it. Would you like a beer right now? Grab one. You like dancing? Do a little jig. Want to share your life intimately with someone? Get married. Listen to a good song you both like, and go see a good movie together.

Actions and character really matter, not rules.

I just don't think God cares all that much about some of the rules we put together. I really do believe he gives us free will and leaves our choices up to us. Yes, he may at times be like a disappointed father whose kids have overeaten on Thanksgiving Day. He loves us and knows what's best for us.

Most importantly, I think he wants us to follow him and live passionately. So, I guess we have to imagine what kind of people we want to be, visualize the kind of futures we want to create, and then come up with the parameters and strategies that will help us stay on track. And, ultimately, remember that we have to live with the consequences of our choices, good or bad.

Mostly, that's how I see rules: they help me stay on track and, hopefully, become a better person.

And since I still hate them at times, I try to remember that rules are there to protect my devotion and deepen my love.

So, follow the rules. Or don't. It's your own *damn* choice.

#6 Love

It plays out the same every time. My wife sits down with the kids and I take their orders. Aiden: chicken nugget Happy Meal. Logan: Happy Meal with a cheeseburger. Carson: drool and small pieces of our bread (he's still a baby). Lisa: Quarter Pounder and small Sprite.

This is where it starts. It's been ten years and it hasn't changed. I know my wife loves fries. So, I ask, "No fries?" Of course, I already know her answer: "No. I'm not that hungry." And I know another thing: I *am* hungry and I want *all* my fries.

Why do I say that? Without fail, halfway through her cheeseburger, she'll start picking at my fries like a seagull scavenging on the busy summer beach. Oh yeah, she also starts sipping my Coke. Refills on Coke are free, so that's no big deal. But refills on fries are not. That's a big deal.

This is a delicate situation. With all my strength, I try to be aware of my body language and control it. I casually ask, "Do you want me to go get you some fries?"

"No. I don't want any."

I keep quiet. But I'm thinking, *Then why are you eating all my frickin' fries?*

And she knows what I'm thinking. She calls me on it: "Why don't you like sharing?" Or, "Why are you so selfish?" Sometimes both for emphasis.

I politely smile, let out a half-chuckle, and counter with, "Selfish? I want to do the most generous thing possible and buy you your *own* fries. How can I possibly share any more than that?" I try to ooze charm in my delivery. It's a good comeback, but she never buys it.

My wife is without doubt the most important person in the world to me. Marrying her has made me a better man. It's the second-best decision I've ever made. But I can't stand it when someone eats off my plate and drinks from my cup. I can't explain why. It's not that I'm a germ freak or anything. I don't find it gross. But it absolutely drives me up the wall. Even now, as I think about it, I'm cringing. As important as Lisa is to me, as much as I love her, she isn't spared that quirk of mine.

The Beatles had an instant hit when they sang *All You Need Is Love*. And I believed it for a long time. But it's not true. Share my fries with the one I love? No way. Let her put her cold hands on my back to warm them up on a crisp winter day? Get away.

So, what's the problem?

This isn't something that just clicked for me. I didn't have a moment of clarity and finally get it. This is something I am still learning.

I think we know the problem, and we don't like admitting it. I do, and I hate admitting it.

Learning about love has been an ongoing process, something I've had to suffer through many times. Sure, there's great irony in having a chapter here on hating love. It's not that I hate love in and of itself. Who in his right mind would? I love *being* loved, as we all do. That's not the issue.

More accurately, it's *loving* I hate. I hate having to always *be* loving. I hate having to be loving toward people I'd much rather ignore. I hate to love like Jesus taught, modeled, and prayed that we would all imitate. To truly love, I always have to be "on." I hate having to *work* at loving. I hate the process and practice of what Jesus laid out. I'd much rather love who I want, when I want.

I'd much rather go with the *feeling* called love. If I feel it, I'll do it. If I don't, I won't. That's easier. But that's emotion, not love.

If there's one thing the life of Jesus taught us, it's that love is a choice. It seems like it shouldn't be so much work, but it is. A lot of the time, we just have to muscle through it.

Love is unnatural that way.

Intro to Love

I'm always on my mind. I have been for a long time. Ever since I can remember, I've been thinking about myself. Most of us do.

When we were still living in South Florida, one of my favorite things to do on my day off was to pack up the kids and head over to Barnes & Noble. They had a children's section in the back of the store with an incredible Thomas the Train table. It had everything — bridges, water station, and trains galore. Our kids would play, and we would read. It was relaxing, so long as the kids cooperated.

So, on the way to the bookstore, we would prepare them. The you-need-to-share-with-the-other-boys-and-girls lecture would ensue. It helped them get in the right mindset, since my oldest liked to hog all the trains.

On one particular day there were kids everywhere, and my oldest, then three and a half, was being a poster child for diplomacy. As kids came to the table, he would say, "What's your name? You wanna train?" At one point, he'd given them all away, and he didn't even care. Eventually the other kids left, and he had every train to himself. So there he was pushing them all.

I was proud and took the opportunity to tell him. But I reminded him he would still have to share when more kids came. Then he had his own little moment. He paused and reflected. With his bright green eyes sparkling, he shared his epiphany: "Daddy, I don't have to share with the other boys and girls. I'm already sharing with myself!" I laughed out loud. He'd just given me the definitive explanation of selfish.

Being selfish is natural. Being selfless is not. It's why we learn to say "mine" before most other words and use it more often.

All I think about is what to do with my time, my money, and my possessions concerning *ME*. Where I invest these things clearly exposes what I care about, what I love.

I once spent days trying to figure out where to get a part for my vintage truck. After finally locating it, I spent another day getting it from a junkyard several hours away. Then I brought it to the mechanic and spent a bunch of money to have it installed. Later that week, my wife asked me to get her some water while we watched

TV. I sighed and reluctantly got it. Obviously, this didn't make her feel loved. She asked how I could go so far for my truck, yet resent going such a short distance to get her a glass of water. I knew I was wrong.

To make matters worse, our culture's literature, movies, poems, songs, and the like constantly reinforce our self-love. "Love your-self," they insist. "Make sure you're happy." But happily ever after isn't real life. Surrendering to that whimsical emotion is reckless and selfish. What do I do when the rush wears off (because it always does)? Do I set out to conquer a *new* love and ignore the conse-quences of this pattern?

So, I've had to unlearn and then relearn what it means to love. And it hasn't been easy.

Love 101: Unconditional

Of course, we all know love should be unconditional. You probably knew I was going to say that. But it's true. *Unconditional* is what love has to be.

I build that understanding of love on the meaning of the word itself. In the New Testament, four different Greek terms are trans-lated as *love* in our English Bibles. Each has a different connotation. One of them, *agape,* indicates a selfless love that isn't sexual in nature. It implies a love that's active, regardless of reciprocation.

Agape is the word Jesus used when he said we should love our neighbors as ourselves and then illustrated that in his story of the Good Samaritan.[17] He told about a man on a journey who was robbed, beaten, and left to die on the roadside. Two other travelers, a teacher of the Jewish law and a religious leader, passed him by.

The only person to stop and help was a Samaritan—a man from a despised ethnic group. So, which of those three travelers showed love to that dying man? The answer's obvious.

Elsewhere in the New Testament, we're taught to show *agape* love to children, the poor, the sick, spouses, neighbors, friends, God, and even enemies—anyone and everyone. The desirable, less desirable, and undesirable—all are to be loved like this.

Jesus defined *agape* love when he said, "Love one another the way I loved you."[18] Jesus loved selflessly. He loved without expectation. He loved unconditionally. It's one thing to have sympathy, or even empathy, for someone else, but Jesus tells us to take it to the next level.

When I think of this selfless love, I think of my friend Mat. I've known him since ninth grade. He married his high school sweetheart. They left their wedding reception and drove off to college to live on love. He likes to eat (like me), and he's brilliant (unlike me). What's great about our friendship is that we've never been at odds—except once.

Like a good best man, I decorated his car when they got married. I wrote all over it with shoe polish. Well, I thought it was shoe polish. It was actually that stuff that takes out scuffs, and I didn't realize it was permanent. The black writing over the light cream color of his car really stood out.

Mat said the congratulatory honking was funny at first, but got old after a few months. Then they were cited by their apartment complex and were forced to repaint the car. It took a month of their income. He says I still owe him.

He and his wife have three special-needs children. They were foster children at first, but Mat and his wife couldn't bear the thought of losing them, so they adopted them. That meant they gave up oodles of state funds, but it didn't matter.

Two of these kids have had terminal sicknesses since birth. Mat and his wife knew it, but that didn't stop them. One day soon, these children they've spent their time, efforts, and money on will die. Their time together could end any day. In addition, their other child is mute, blind, and quadriplegic. Can you imagine?

They decided they're going to show love to these children, though others might not. They took these kids in and made them their own. No matter the cost. No matter the loss.

That's what unconditional love is. That's how we're to love.

Love 201: Others

Jesus not only said to love your neighbor as yourself, but he also taught what's known as the Golden Rule: treat others the same way you want them to treat you.[19] I like to blend these two commands and simply say, *Love others the way you want to be loved*. Since I like to be first, according to this application, I should learn to put others first—and to express that love in ways that I like it expressed to me. This means not always saying everything I'm thinking or getting what I want or doing what I want or going where I want to go.

Furthermore, I take this to mean we all need each other. I've been prone to walk away from relationships and cut people off when they make me mad. When I don't feel like loving others, I'm tempted to avoid them altogether. But I've never met someone who's actually happier (or even happy at all) because of cutting off or avoiding relationships to escape being hurt, let down, taken advantage of, or whatever. That doesn't work. We need each other. So, we have to live like it.

I remember taking our kids to see a movie last year, and we showed up early to get good seats. There we were, sitting with our preschoolers waiting for our G-rated film to start. Before the movie, and even before the regular previews, they showed a promotional spot for an upcoming flick that featured fighting, swords, axes, blood, and big scary warriors who looked like monsters. I was seething inside. I looked at my wife, who was equally ticked off. We sat up, ready to walk out and demand to speak to the manager. We'd tell him, "We're sick of this assault on our children's innocence!" We'd get our money back, while also mentioning that we would be contacting the movie company and all their partners, parent companies, and affiliates. This was outrageous. It was war, and we were ready to fight!

Then the real previews started and…you know…they're always so good. We just love watching them. Plus, the movie was about to start. And we'd just gotten everyone settled with buttered popcorn, candy, and Sprite (Coke for me, of course). And it's so hard to plan time like this together. So, we agreed to deal with this *after* the movie.

Well, we didn't. By then, we'd cooled off and decided not to push it. Besides, there's always the feeling it won't really make any difference. That's what I tell myself when I want to avoid conflict. In the moment, it's just easier to go away and leave it alone.

Avoiding a conflict at a movie theater with a manager is one thing, but avoiding others because there may be conflict is another. In relationships, we can't just cut and run.

Sometimes you avoid confrontations in your closest relationships because you're told that if you *really* love someone, and the relationship is really meant to be, you'll never fight with each other. But that's a load of crap.

Or maybe you've been in a troubled relationship, and you're thinking, *I've tried working through everything with so-and-so, but it doesn't seem to help. What do I do?* I admit there are times—in an effort not to make things worse, and when you've done everything possible to work things out—when it's best to part ways until another day. Sometimes people just can't work through an issue. That's not to say there's no solution. It just means either one or both people involved in the conflict won't do all it takes to find it. Maybe they don't clearly see their own issues, or can't move past the wrongs done to them. We just need to make sure we've done all we can to make amends, to reconcile, to ask for forgiveness, and to grant forgiveness, no matter the price.

We can't forget how much we need each other. We're to love everyone the way we want to be loved—those who are like us and those who aren't. Those who agree with us and those who don't. Those who are lovable and those who aren't. Those who are healthy and those who are sick. Those who are rich and those who are poor. Even that guy down the street who has a huge house and three times more yard than anyone else, who drives a luxury car during the week and a Harley Davidson on the weekend, and whom I seem to dislike for no reason at all—even *he* deserves to be loved, though he seems to have everything he could possibly need.

It's the way of things. It's the way of love.

Love others the way you want to be loved.

Love 301: Enemies

I really hate this part. There are many people we can view as enemies. Maybe it's someone who stole money from us, who rubbed us the wrong way, who jockeyed us out of a promotion at work, or who abused us. Typically, we think of doing bad things to our enemies for revenge. While that would be so satisfying, Jesus had a different idea.

Jesus admonishes his followers with this direct command: "Love your enemies." He immediately breaks that down for us: *"Do good to those who hate you, bless those who curse you, pray for those who are cruel to you."* [20] The nerve of him!

One of the most amazing things about my father is that, as long as I can remember, he has never had an enemy. People like that are rare, and I'm fortunate to be related to one. I'm not quite as patient and accepting as he is. In fact, not even close. I have enemies. Quite a few, I suppose. At least I have the memory of how my father treated people that were difficult to deal with. It helps me understand what Jesus meant, at least in a relational sense, when he gave that difficult challenge to love our enemies.

But I still find this principle confusing. Obviously, there must be a context to it. I could be wrong, but I don't think Jesus is telling me to be a pacifist. I don't want to be a doormat and never defend others or myself.

For Christmas, I bought my kids remote-controlled tanks that shoot plastic BB's, and I dress the boys up in long sleeves and hats and goggles so they can shoot each other. When I told my aunt, she was appalled. She said, "I thought you were a pacifist!" I was insulted. When I related her comment to a friend, he responded by saying he thinks every pacifist should get beat up at least once. That cracked me up.

There's no way I'm going to resort to pacifism if some guy breaks into my house and tries to tie up my family and me. I'm going to do all I can to distract him so I can grab the meat cleaver and bury it in his chest. I know that's a little graphic, but I have a wife and three children, and I think I have to love them before I love someone like that. Call me crazy, but I won't be wasting time trying to negotiate with him.

Jesus wasn't a pacifist. That may be a shock to you, because he's often portrayed as one. I, too, was surprised to find out he once got violent with a bunch of people—two times, actually. On both occasions he saw religious leaders in the Jewish temple that were taking advantage of people trying to reconnect with God. So, Jesus took care of business. He made a whip (which took quite a while) and then started turning the place upside-down, yelling all the while.[21] I don't know any self-respecting pacifist who would act in such a premeditated, violent manner.

It's funny to visualize. He's sitting there, making that whip, maybe thinking, "I'm so tired of these guys disrespecting my dad (God). Boy are they gonna get it! I'm going to walk right in there in the middle of them all and beat the stink out of every one of them. I'm gonna tell them not to come back until they're ready to apologize and get right with God!" I might be embellishing, but it can't be too much of a stretch.

I think the lesson here is that sometimes "tough love" appears extreme, but is actually much needed. Sometimes the most loving thing to do is to enforce some type of discipline in order to stop what's happening or prevent something worse. In this case, Jesus didn't want people to have the wrong impression of God. In today's world, it may be the parents who kick out their eighteen-year-old who's caught up in illegal activities. Sometimes we can have tough love without actually making enemies. Sometimes we just have to make hard decisions.

Of course, looking further at Jesus' life, he didn't defend himself or take any violent action to keep from being crucified. He did seem more like a pacifist as the soldiers spat on him, beat him with their fists, whipped him nearly to death, put a crown of thorns on his head, and finally crucified him. He didn't fight back. In fact, he didn't say a word against them. So there's obviously some context and timing when it comes to loving your enemies. I just haven't figured it out yet.

I think when we categorize people as enemies they die to us. It deposits bitterness in our hearts, and this tends to grow. That's not a healthy thing to carry around—the anger and unresolved tension. It's a burden, and it can lead us to pull away from other relationships, even healthy ones.

Treating someone as an enemy can be something as simple as honking at a driver who cuts you off in traffic or hanging up on a telephone solicitor before he gets a word out. These people can be subtle enemies in our minds, but they still deserve a certain level of respect.

The best way for me to understand how to love my enemies is to put it into the context of relationship. I suppose Jesus is admonishing us to work out whatever conflict there is while there's a chance to work it out. And along the way, to defend the innocent whenever possible—making sure not to misrepresent God's character in the process.

Love 401: Forgiveness

If love is like a big circle, forgiveness is the final arc that completes it.

Or maybe that's too poetic. Perhaps love's more like a sandwich. *Unconditional* is the top piece of bread, *others* and *enemies* are the filling, and *forgiveness* is on the bottom holding it all together. (Food always has a sense of poetry to me.)

Love isn't truly whole without forgiveness. As strange as it may sound, it's possible to be kind toward people without forgiving them for wrongs they've done to you. It's even possible to forgive and not be particularly nice about it, as if you're making the other person pay a little. Forgiveness takes love beyond the surface. It's huge.

Forgiveness plays such a vital role because every relationship you're part of will fall short and let you down. It's strange how easy it is to resent people you're supposed to care about because they won't be who you want them to be or do what you want them to do. It seems like the habit of hating catches on much quicker than the habit of loving.

In every relationship, no matter who it is, you're going to be hurt on some level at some point. You won't have an expectation met, you won't get something you need, and you won't feel valued or respected to the degree you want. All this adds stress. As the cycle continues, this tension can eventually damage the relationship and even ruin it if the strain is left untreated.

The only way to fix this is to forgive. Forgiveness releases the burden and repairs the damage to the bond.

Failure to forgive is death to any relationship. Underlying unforgiveness brings frustration. This will eventually lead to anger, then bitterness, and then a hardened heart. It's the absolute opposite of love.

Unforgiveness is like weeds. Weeds take over. It's their nature.

The previous owner of our house was an old guy who couldn't really care for the yard too well. The weeds took over an entire half-acre and grew to about six feet tall. I tried to clean it up. Weed-killer wouldn't do it. I even bought the good stuff, the make-it-a-barren-wastcland stuff. I went through a couple gallons, to no avail. I finally had to hire professionals to clear out my yard.

Like those weeds, unforgiveness grows around our hearts and sucks out the life in us. It kills the connections you try to maintain with others. However, forgiveness breathes new life into those bonds.

I know it's hard sometimes, especially when there have been harsh words or even abuse. But forgiving is the right thing to do. Everybody has some pain, hurt, and brokenness that love can heal to some degree. A heart that moves toward reconciliation keeps itself from turning hard and bitter. It moves away from unforgiveness.

But forgiveness still confuses me. First, it's not a one-time thing. It has to be a mindset. It has to be a predetermined approach to relationships. It's as if we say from the beginning, "I know I'll be hurt or even wronged in the pursuit of this relationship, since you are imperfect and may not meet my standards or expectations. So I plan on having to be a forgiving person if this is going to work at all." I hate that.

Also, complete forgiveness is a two-part process — like a two-way street. It involves both the person who asks for it and the person who grants it. Sometimes you may ask and not get it; sometimes you may grant it even though you haven't been asked.

Forgiveness repairs the damage created by the messiness of life. Forgiving means loving someone completely, regardless of flaws, regardless of wrongs. Incidentally, forgiveness like this is what Jesus did for our relationship with our Creator, to reconnect us with him. There's nothing more loving or more Godlike than to forgive.

Forgiveness is love's highest level. It's also the most difficult, and the hardest love lesson to learn, especially when someone has really hurt you. To forgive is divine.

Love 501: Confusion

Sometimes love, even forgiving love, is more confusing.

I carry a lot of baggage. I don't like it, but it's there. Plus, I have a problem with anger, as you may have suspected. I also have a problem with forgiveness. I carry these things around more than I like to admit. I hate that I can never seem to forget things. Although I'm an adult, I can't get over certain experiences. It's not that I don't want to. But I'm often reminded of the past in the present. It's not that I want to live in the past. I just hate having to relive it in the present.

That's where I am with my mom. I usually don't handle this relationship well at all. I want to love her better. And even though I've written an entire chapter about this stuff, mostly I still don't know how.

In respect to my mother, I want to make it clear that what I'm about to say is my perspective and it's probably wrong. It's based on how *I* feel. Rather than unbiased reality, it's how *I* assess the facts, what is real to me. This is a part of my family dynamic. (I'm sure my mom could give you a long list about me too.) My parents divorced when I was an infant. As far as I can tell, based on conflicting accounts from the two of them, I went back and forth between my mom and dad until I was about two or three. From then on, I was with my dad, and my mother wasn't around.

Her gifts to me were usually a month or so late. She never came to see me, but I visited her for a few weeks every year. When I was young, I would often cry on the flight back after visiting her (kids were allowed to travel alone back then). I don't know why I cried. I just did. I couldn't control it.

I try to understand how fortune wasn't kind to her in life, as she says, and that this is the explanation for her absence. But I really don't get it. She wasn't physically or mentally handicapped or in jail.

Over the last couple of years, my wife and I have made a concerted effort to make her part of our lives, mainly for the sake of our kids. We want them to grow up with family around. So, we talked her into living near us. We think that's how it should be, but it's not easy.

When it comes to abrasiveness, negativity, and tactlessness, she's in the hall of fame. There are also her tendencies to cuss and smoke like a trucker. I remember when she finally visited my wife and me one Christmas in Florida before we had kids. We were with all our friends and their kids on Christmas Day. The house was full, and we were all having a great time talking and snacking while waiting for dinner. But my wife and I never got to eat the Christmas ham. My mom decided to add to the lighthearted conversation by discussing a study she'd read on AIDS and anal sex. There were preschoolers playing in the room. I was furious and so embarrassed. We left.

She thinks she knows everything about everything. She always knows how to do it better. She could cook tastier Cajun salmon than Emeril. She could run a school better than the dean. She could run a social program better than any professional social worker. All of which she has relatively little or no experience in, let alone measurable success from my point of view.

She's never at a loss to tell me what I should be doing as a parent, since she's better at that than I am. If I need to discipline one of my kids, she'll interfere. She'll say, "But you need to know *why* he did it!" No, I don't. I don't care why he sassed his mother. I don't care if he slept too little, ate too much, stubbed his toe, or whatever. He simply isn't allowed to talk to her like that. Of course, Mom insists I'm wrong.

When my kids come back from her house, they're sleep deprived. They have diarrhea from eating too much junk. And they have terrible attitudes that take days to adjust.

She has a way of breaking things. I once loaned her my radio. It came back broken. Another time I lent her a pair of pliers. Also broken. (A difficult task, mind you.) I always have to fix what she breaks.

She's militant too. She's on a mission to subdue men—a feminist through and through. She affectionately refers to herself as a *feminazi*. If there's a problem, no matter what it is, it's because of a man. Specifically, all the world's problems are due to rich, white men. While that may be true in certain contexts, it has nothing to do with why her lawnmower won't run or why the pool company won't honor the warranty on her pump. They won't come because she cussed at them on the phone and threatened to sue. And by the way, if we're going to be honest, rich, white men are generally the ones fixing problems and funding the solutions. As a percentage of the whole, they're investing the most time and money when there's a need. They're usually the philanthropists.

She loves her pets though. She always has. She has four dogs and three cats and she feeds the birds in the yard. I call it a domestic farm. Her pets are people to her. She's always had lots of pets. In fact, over the years, she's been more faithful and devoted to them than she has been to me, her only child.

Nearly every time I see her, one of three things happens (sometimes all three):

She calls me "stupid," or something like it.

She calls me something more colorful, like "ass." Of course, she denies this. She'll say, "I didn't say you *are* an ass; I said you're *acting like* an ass." That logic might hold up in a courtroom slander trial, but not in a real relationship.

If she's in a lighter mood, she'll belittle something I believe, a core value I have, or my perspective on something.

I try to get along with my mom, but mostly I don't. The relationship is draining for me. She expects me to give her special treatment. Out of frustration with me, she often protests, "I'm your *mother!*" But that just doesn't mean much. It's hard to fabricate the emotion. The investment wasn't there; the respect from her isn't there, so the credibility and influence are holding on by a thread. It *can* be there;

it will just take time to build.

Her expectations are hard to live up to. Even now, when she's generous, particularly with money, it always comes back as her leverage to win an argument or to try to manipulate me into doing something on her house that absolutely cannot wait. It's not like I don't have anything else going on—running and working in my own business, being married, having three kids, having my own house that always needs work, being involved at my church, and trying to write a book in my free time. Somehow, she didn't need me before in her life, but now I'm indispensable and responsible for fixing her woes.

It's hard, because she refuses to change anything about herself. She's proud of who she is. In fact, I think she may feel that changing would be compromising her "true self," the person she "really" is. I view change and adapting as part of what it means to "have a relationship" and to "learn to coexist." But those phrases aren't in her book of life skills, at least not that I see.

I'm not sure why it's like this. I'm not the nicest, most patient guy in the world, but I don't think I've done anything to merit the full force and weight all this brings. Maybe I was a mistake because my arrival was accidental. Maybe I remind her of a time, circumstances, and people she'd like to forget. Maybe I remind her of unfulfilled hopes and dreams. Maybe her plans were sidetracked. Or maybe it's just because I own man parts.

I say all that to say: *None of it matters*. It doesn't matter in respect to love in its full measure. Love tries to forget and works to forgive. I hate that part. Because, mostly, I fail. And, honestly, I'd much rather avoid all the energy it takes.

Love is work. It always will be. Although I may not always feel that loving emotion, I try to be loving in my actions. And there's only one reason I do. There's only one reason I continue to work through the relationship, only one reason why I see any value in having my mom be part of our lives and our kids' lives. There's only one reason I don't give up and take the easier path. It's because of what Jesus did for me, for us. It's because of what Jesus modeled in love and forgiveness that I do any of this.

I know it's the right thing to do. I know it's the closest thing to unconditional love I'm able to achieve. And looking back over the recent past, we've made some progress. Not much, but some.

Sure, I would rather keep a long record of wrongs I feel were done to me. It would be easier to hold grudges and never forget. I would love to demand restitution from everyone who has ever wronged me. But that's no way to live. That's not love. That's not living.

Love Is...

In the movie *Forrest Gump,* the main character lived by the phrase *Stupid is as stupid does.* Though you may have an IQ of 75, like he did, you're limited only by what you choose to let limit you. The funny thing is, because he was simple, he wasn't hung up on the things most of us are. He lived a life of monumental achievements because he was too dumb to realize he couldn't do them.

Maybe we should look at love like that.

Keep it simple: *Love is as love does.* It's a good measure. The only limits are the ones we set for it.

Simple love is a good description of Jesus. It's there not only in his dying for us—*the* defining act of love—but also in how he gave of himself totally to others in his daily life. He's our best example of love.

But I still hate having to love everyone. It disrupts my life. It costs me something—getting my way or what I want. Love can cost money and even cause you to lose sleep. It may be the reason your hopes and dreams are on hold. It may be why you have to settle sometimes. But nothing's more important in this life than love. Life minus love equals zero.

You don't have to like everyone. But you do have to love, whether you derive measurable benefit from it or not or whether a person seems worth it or not or whether you are loved back or not. You have to love, because it's love or nothing.

The apostle Paul, the primary writer of the New Testament, gives us the right picture in these words: *"I gain nothing if I do not have love. Love is patient and kind. Love is not jealous, it does not brag, and it's not proud. Love is not rude, is not selfish, and does not get upset with others. Love does not count up wrongs that have been done. Love takes no pleasure in evil but rejoices over the truth. Love patiently accepts all things. It always trusts, always hopes, and always endures. Love never ends."*[22]

That's an amazing definition. And it's the challenge of the whole lesson on love in all its fullness. Love is a choice. It's hard work. It can be frustrating, exhausting, inconvenient, and drive you to your limits.

I guess we don't *have* to love everyone—but it's worth a try. It makes us better people and the world a better place.

Love is as love does. Just like Jesus did. Love like this is a miracle.

#6 Love

#7 Hell

I remember my first horror movie. It was R-rated, I was only five, and my father took me to see it. My mother still holds it against him. At this, he's quick to recall that in that same year she took me to see an intense murder mystery while I was visiting her. Ah, the baggage…

Anyway, it was *Invasion of the Body Snatchers*. Aliens take over the world by replacing humans with exact alien copies. Looking back, it was laughable. But at the time, it haunted me, especially the image of one cloning gone bad—a dog with a human face. I couldn't sleep for weeks.

I also remember seeing the first horror movie I liked when I was a little older. It was called *The Thing*. Scientific explorers discover an alien spacecraft in Antarctica that's been frozen in ice for millennia. When they thawed it out, an alien creature came alive and starting taking over and making human hosts of everyone. The result was an explosion of blood and guts giving way to this new abomination.

I'm no expert, but I think every successful horror film has a singular purpose, and it's not to be gross. The grossness simply helps accomplish the goal.

Any horror movie worth its weight in screams and gore uses the monster to reveal what's truly lurking within. As the characters feel trapped and isolated with no apparent way out, the impending doom exposes their true qualities. Sometimes self-serving characters transform into sacrificing heroes. Or characters you like at first end up leaving everyone behind to save themselves. The monster without reveals the monster—or the savior—within.

Horror films are primal, with little pretense, and they quickly get to the point of illuminating true character. That's why I love them. The evil is easily identifiable. And I think the evil portrayed in horror movies perfectly matches what hell is to Christianity. The idea of hell reveals a lot about the Christian faith and those who believe in it.

It's no secret that hell is probably the most uncomfortable aspect of the Christian faith. For many years I was content to ignore it and simply think, *Everyone goes to heaven.* When that stopped making sense—in light of the evident evil in this world—my conclusion evolved into this: Good people go to heaven, bad people go to hell. But that started to break down, too, as I realized that "good" is measured on a sliding scale, and everyone has a different standard. Some twisted minds even view obvious evil actions as good.

I realized I had to do some more investigating of this idea of hell, though I wondered what good could come from it. To say that I hate hell, and that I especially hate talking about it, is a huge understatement. But if I'm going to find the true value in the teachings and person of Jesus (and the Bible), I have to deal with this issue.

Resident Evil

Generally, I've found that people think of hell in one of three ways: as a place, as a state (or condition) we create, or as separation from God.

Probably the most common view is that hell's a place—some kind of afterlife destination—and the abode of immeasurable suffering and pain. No one would want to go there.

This is the view of hell I heard Christians yelling about on several street corners when I was visiting Chicago. It's also what I was berated with coming out of the train station in Atlanta many years ago with my tattoos and earrings. Hell was revealing the monster in those who were yelling at me.

It made me wonder why a belief in something so serious didn't bring more compassion and concern. "Turn or burn!" just didn't seem like something Jesus would say to people who might be spiritually lost. Shock value tactics just don't appear to promote long-term devotion in any arena of life.

In the Bible, there does seem to be a common thread of hell being a place. In the Old Testament, it's seen as the depths of the earth, the farthest point from heaven, a place like a prison with no return, a pit or a grave, and a place of torment, judgment, and death.[23]

Jesus also talked a lot about hell. He described it as a place of torment, of burning, of destruction, of condemnation, of fire, of "outer darkness," and of "burning sulfur."[24] In one particularly striking image, he told the story of a man looking up from the torments of hell and craving the simple relief of just one cool drop of water on his tongue.[25] We also learn from Jesus that hell was originally designed for the devil and his demons, not for human beings.[26] But like the devil and his demons, humanity became part of this equation by rejecting God.

The Bible ends in the book of Revelation with Jesus handing out final judgments for all of creation. Meanwhile, the devil, his fallen angels, and anyone whose name isn't found in "the book of life" are thrown into "a lake of fire."[27] Some refer to this as the Judgment Day, a term that conjures up a host of emotions. (See why I hate talking about hell?)

We're not told when all this will happen, but when it does, God will redefine life as we know it for his people. A new age will start with a new way of living—free from evil, pain, and suffering[28]— just the way God initially created our existence to be when there was no evil in the world (before the first sin). Meanwhile, before the Judgment Day comes, we all have the option to choose whether or not to follow God.

I have some thoughts that don't sit well with this view of hell. If hell is literal and the result of not deciding to follow God (specifically, not to follow Jesus), then why do so many of the statements referring to hell, including Jesus' own words, seem to be associated more with our behavior than with a specific decision not to believe in Jesus?

I suppose the argument could be made that our behavior is a reflection of what we believe, which I would agree with. But what about all those people who call themselves "Christians," but do whatever they want? Are they saved from hell? Their behavior would say otherwise.

I've also noticed that this view of hell conveys a type of elitism. Christians have a tendency to come off as cliquish and arrogant. They'll offer the message of Jesus as a *Get Out of Hell Free* card. This may explain why so many of them go on living however they want. They have their cards, they're hell-insured, and forgiveness is free, so there are no restrictions. When challenged on this, some Christians even reply, "Once saved, always saved." That doesn't seem sincere. Our actions must matter on some level.

But I want to be fair. There's an unavoidable tension when we're considering the idea of some people being condemned to a lake of fire for eternity. No matter how kind and encouraging a Christian might be when asked about hell in this context, it will sound harsh, mean, and even exclusive. No amount of sugar will help that medicine go down smoother.

It's just not a pleasant subject, and I hate it.

Hell Raiser

Another view sees hell as more of a state or condition. Which brings to mind the worst job I ever had.

While I was in college, I served as a helper in a daycare program. After classes, I would shoot over for a few hours to help watch these K-through-8th grade kids. My coworker and I mainly played kickball and video games with them and put puzzles together.

They hired me because they said they needed a strong male. It was supposed to be easy, but it was bad. Real bad. What they really needed was lots of duct tape and rope for those wild animals.

The kids were incorrigible. Every day was chaos. Like elephants stampeding through the jungle, they didn't listen.

I remember one time all the kids were gravitating toward the tree line on the edge of the property. I finally walked over to see what all the commotion was about. I couldn't believe my eyes. One kid was on the ground encircled by three others who were beating him with broken-off tree limbs. It was like a gang initiation you'd see on TV. All the other kids were just curiously watching and doing nothing.

But whenever the school's director would come near, the kids would miraculously change, as if suddenly transported to some magical fantasyland. When she was around, they said things like "please," "thank you," and "yes ma'am." They even cleaned up their messes when asked the first time. For some reason, they listened to her—and I was jealous. I couldn't create a fantasy world there of my own.

What my coworker and I managed to create was a total nightmare. Yet our boss—just by showing up—made it into something utopian, complete with children giggling and birds chirping in the cool breeze. One reality was chaotic and miserable; the other was blissful and calm.

The second concept of hell is a lot like that. Hell isn't defined as a specific place and neither is heaven. Each is more of a "type" than an actual place. And each is something we create, based on our decisions and how we live. We're responsible for either creating or preventing it. Our actions in this life— how we live, what we do with our resources, time, talents, experience, etc.— will eventually bring about either a state of heaven or a state of hell. So we as human beings have a certain level of control over what heaven or hell ends up looking like for us.

It's a lot like karma. It's that simple.

This view of hell is loosely based on all the same passages that seem to point to a "place" called hell. But this second view interprets those passages less literally and more metaphorically.

Ultimately, this view begs the question of why Jesus came to earth. It's said that he came to teach us a new way to live, a way in which we have the means, knowledge, and model (in Jesus' example) to create this state of heaven. We're to teach others this way and contribute to the greater good in this world. We are to redeem our own broken existences through our actions and teach others how to do the same. These changes will bring about something heavenly as we corporately affect the world. At least that's the goal.

But then, why was Jesus killed? For being a good example?

It's thought that what Jesus said was so countercultural, and such a departure from the religious thinking of the day, he was declared a heretic. His death was the consequence of his theological and civil disobedience in the religiously theocratic culture of the day.

By this point I reach my limitations and get a little lost with this particular view. It sounds a little like Eastern religions. I'm not sure if that's good or bad, but I'm confused nonetheless. It seems to break down a little in the details.

Does Jesus really even matter in this context? Did he really come to die simply to teach us some good stuff? Is that really something to die for? What he did seems a little more important than that, as if there was something *really, really* bad he wanted to spare us from.

There's also the question of how the Judgment Day events

described in Revelation fit into this view of hell. Are these events purely metaphorical, representing something else? Have they already happened somehow? And I don't really understand where the devil and all his demons fit into this. Maybe hell and the lake of fire are specifically for them and no one else—a time when God eventually removes all evil from this world.

Taking it a step further, if being good and making the world better is the goal, wouldn't it be more effective to leave off any mention of God or Jesus? Since discussing God and Jesus can so often be divisive, why not create a new secular humanist faith that avoids all that? One that's totally dedicated to promoting good deeds and good will among all. This would probably be more readily accepted. Coexistence and harmony between all creation—man, animals, and environment—would create universal peace and a heavenly state. Who could argue with that? This less offensive, more congenial religion would probably have more impact on society and culture as a whole.

All we have to do is leave God and Jesus out of the equation.

This idea brings to mind a host of other questions. But the main thing, as I understand this particular view of hell, is that it's a state or condition that we ourselves are responsible for creating or preventing.

Good luck.

The Haunting

I would describe the final concept of hell as separation from God.

From this perspective, nothing's worse than being damned to spend eternity away from your Creator. There may or may not be burning and flames, but there's certainly no peace.

In this hell, people suffer because there's never the comfort of encouraging words or the healing, intimate embrace from their heavenly Father. There's no true healing from the troubles of life and the pains endured there. There are no resolutions. The people blew it by rejecting God, and in the end got exactly what they wanted: God nowhere close.

Those in this hell will never have contentment; the things they sought in their earthly lives will consume them for eternity. Their selfish ambitions, addictions, and appetites will eat at them forever. There'll never be victory in this struggle.

Sometimes we hear that it's good to let a struggling person hit bottom, and that the unrestrained natural consequences of wrong choices are sometimes the best teachers. The thought is that the road to recovery begins at the bottom—when the person is finally ready to look up.

But in this hell, there's no relief. You're perpetually hitting bottom. Actually, there is no bottom. You can never see out of your own misery. As much as you may cry out to God, there's no respite. Whatever you consumed (and whatever consumed you) in life will be your torment in hell. From then on, the thing that kept you from turning to God will be the only thing you get. And it will not even bring the temporary pleasure that it sometimes did in life.

I've also heard it mentioned that part of the horror in this environment will be the constant moans and screams of the damned as they call out to God in their misery.

This picture of hell also stirs some odd musings for me. It pretty much seems like the "time-out" discipline our kids get, but on a big, cosmic, permanent scale, and where your destructive appetites aren't allowed to be satisfied. Is that really so bad? Will the possibility of something like this as the consequence for our actions really cause people to change their lives for the better? Will it really bring a sense of urgency to follow God?

As a parent, I've learned that time-outs have their limitations. When my boys are sitting in time-outs, I'll often observe them from around the corner, only to see they have many ways to entertain themselves. They sit there fully engaged in their own little games, patterns, and rhythms that involve wiggling their toes or jumbling their fingers or winking their eyes.

If separation from God is the basic punishment, I don't see the big deal. Some people might even reason that they *like* the idea of being consumed by their appetites for all of eternity. Like one big, long party.

I know plenty of people who are living without God—who don't acknowledge his existence or desire to honor him with their lives— and, to be honest, many of them are happy. It can actually be fun to live with no regard for consequences, able to do whatever we want whenever we want. What's the point of living a life that honors God if there's no sense of a severe consequence for choosing otherwise? People live without God every day. Look around. Are they really all that miserable?

To Hell with It

If you're going to accept that there's a hell, you have to decide: *Is it a place, a self-made condition, or separation from God?*

When the Bible describes hell, is it saying something literal to describe something literal? Or something literal to describe something metaphorical? Or something metaphorical to describe something metaphorical? Or something metaphorical to describe something literal?

Maybe it doesn't matter.

I hate the idea of hell, but perhaps it's not so bad to talk about it. Maybe it's *good* to talk about it. Could it be that all three views are partially true, but none is exclusively correct? In a strange way, I think each view has value, some truth, and important lessons.

Like a storyline in a horror flick, maybe the idea of hell is meant to bring out the best in us, in how we live and how we relate to our surroundings now. I mean, who really lives with a sense of urgency when there's no awareness of consequences? That's why it's easy to be reckless and impulsive as a teenager, when there's not yet an appreciation and respect for outcomes, reciprocity, or pain.

But maybe the bigger issue, and the one that really bothers us, is this: *How could a loving God create hell?*

As brutal as the idea of hell is, it makes sense to me that decisions we make in this life would affect the afterlife. Evil needs to be dealt with. I think everyone would agree with that. But for some reason, there's a departure from this rationale when we add the afterlife element. We don't want it to be true in respect to that. We invent some type of safety-net view of eternity.

It's as if we want to be able to live by our own standards and invent our own senses of morality, but we also want everyone to be rewarded in the end. Like when every kid on every soccer team these days gets a trophy, even the kids that finish in last place. No one's better than anyone else, and no one's s right. Everyone's good in his or her own right. But that just doesn't make sense to me. Hell makes sense.

Should a Mother Teresa be rewarded along with a Hitler just because they both lived sincerely in accordance with their own heartfelt convictions? I can't accept that premise. There must be some standard to figure out and enlighten ourselves with — if there's a God.

Otherwise, God is a liar.

If God is real, how could he be content with a moral vacuum? I'm not. That's why I hate it when true justice doesn't play out in our legal system. But for some reason, I still have a problem accepting the next logical conclusion — that there might be true justice applied in the afterlife.

I certainly don't have a problem accepting the idea that people might be rewarded in the afterlife for the *good* they did on earth. And when it comes to the idea of retribution in the afterlife for wrongdoing, maybe my only reason for squeamishness is selfish. I don't want to get in trouble for the wrong *I've* done, so to let myself off the hook, I let *everyone* off. Everybody gets a trophy!

It's a paradox. Though I can accept the principle of reciprocity, I still want to blame God for carrying it out, as if he's some sort of savage for actually adhering to the principle I want him to stick to.

But really, why *would* a loving God send people to hell? I think that's a loaded question. I like my free will. And if we all truly have it — a certain level of individual autonomy and personal sovereignty — aren't we all really choosing our own destinies, our own consequences? Or instead, should God let everyone off the hook, no matter what he or she has done? Which would be more loving?

I've come to see that in the context of God, it's more loving to have real consequences and true justice. Maybe my concept of God is limited, but I just can't see it any other way. And I've finally decided not to blame God for it.

I don't think God's a liar when he inspired the authors of the Bible to write all they did about hell. How could he possibly want to connect with us, and desire that we honor him with our lives (by being good, helping others, etc.), and then in the end not be that serious about evil and sin? *That* would be a lie to me.

I've also wondered about the possibility that God would use his powers to force people to choose certain things that result in less severe eternal consequences. To me, that's not free will. That would make us more like robots than freethinking beings. Could it be that the most loving thing in the end is to give us all exactly what we wanted? To let us benefit or suffer from our own choices? Isn't that what free will is?

Even in science, there's an equal and opposite reaction to every action; why should this be suspended in the spiritual realm?

Hell Yes!

I've determined that the idea of hell, however we understand it, is *supposed* to make us uncomfortable.

I learned something about this while doing some lay counseling at a past job. Effective counseling is built on the principle that before negative behavior can change, there must be a certain level of pain and discomfort associated with it. Counseling won't work unless the participants realize that what they're doing is hurting others or themselves. If there's no self-awareness, it's a waste of time. If life works like this, why wouldn't the afterlife? Could it be that hell is the grand-scheme, big-picture, eternal application of this principle? Maybe the thought of an eternal sense of discomfort in the afterlife is the only way we'll modify our actions and choices here on earth.

Yes, I do think hell is real. And I lean toward the more literal idea of it. Not because I want to. I'd rather lean toward the metaphor, because it's not as scary. But hell as a place just makes the most sense to me in examining the passages about it in the Bible. Otherwise, I'm leaning on a lot of made-up theory. And where would that end? Soon *all* truth that made me uncomfortable would end up as metaphors. I'd be constantly redefining what Jesus said to make it fit whatever I wanted.

I don't think the details of hell are very important. The issue for me is to take into account how I live this life. Hell helps me care about the bigger picture.

Yes, hell is a monster. And we all have to let the monster reveal who we are. As we think about it, what has hell revealed in us? Anger at God?

Or are we okay with the idea that decisions we make in this life will affect our afterlives? And does that whole concept point us back to Jesus? Just as the horror-flick monster reveals the savior in the hero, hell needs to reveal the savior of the world.

Hell No!

I suppose I've avoided another big question: *How does someone end up in hell?* That's the one no one wants to answer, and it's why we all hate talking about it. That's where my problem with hell all started, so that's where I'll finish.

If you read the account of the life of Jesus, you'll notice he had an annoying habit. He'd often answer a tough question with another question: "I'll answer that if you tell me this…" It was a form of Hebrew debate and banter that challenged higher thinking. This tradition recognized that most people knew the answers to their own questions. Getting them to focus there and verbalize helped them peel away their personal agendas and get to those true answers.

I'm going to be just like Jesus in this, and it may be slightly annoying. I want to emphasize the positive. Jesus said that he didn't come to condemn the world, but to bring life. I want to talk about what it will look like if you end up in heaven, rather than hell—according to Jesus' words.

The last book in the Bible ends with an extraordinary picture of heaven.[29] It shows God living permanently among his people. There's no evil, no temptation, no night. There are no more tears. There's no more death, no more pain. No one will ever be thirsty. No one will ever be hungry. Everything's bright, lighted, brilliant. Precious gems and metals are everywhere. Oceans and rivers are crystal clear to the very bottom. What's rare on this earth is in abundance in heaven.

Of course, we all want to get there. So how do we do it?

The secret, as I've mentioned before, is to have your name recorded in the "book of life."[30]

And how does that happen? I think the answer is found in several passages in the Bible. I'll name just one: *"For God so loved the world that he gave his one and only Son, that whoever believes in him shall not perish but have eternal life. God did not send his Son into the world to condemn the world, but to save the world through him."*[31] If that concept's uncomfortable, don't get mad at me. I'm just the messenger. You'll have to take it up with the one who's quoted as saying this—Jesus. That is, if you believe in such things.

With heaven in the balance, hell does what it's supposed to. It causes me to take stock of my life, examine who I am, challenge what I'm doing, and question why I'm here.

I really don't have a problem accepting that what I do in this life will have eternal ramifications. It's only fair and loving. Or as Maximus expressed in *Gladiator,* "What we do in life echoes in eternity!"

#8 Answers

Good directions can make all the difference.

I remember driving to visit my mom once in the middle of nowhere. Her directions ended with, "Turn right onto the dirt road at the end of the field with about a hundred feet of pine trees." Unfortunately, I arrived at night, when everything was pitch-black. Not to mention, that described the scenery for the last two hours.

Another problem with directions is that there's usually more than one way to get to a place. The question then becomes: *How do we want to get there?* The scenic route? The most direct way? Or maybe the quickest (which may not always be the most direct)?

I think answering a major life question is a lot like that. There's often more than one way to arrive at the answer. And there's usually more than one answer.

I've had many questions for God over the years. I've listed a few of them here, along with some answers based on my experiences and observations. I claim no authority; each one is an answer more than *the* answer. It's simply where I am now and how I arrived there.

I know we all have different answers. That's fine. The point is to keep asking. I hope my effort to find answers will at least drive you to yours.

I am sure of one thing though: we'll all hate some of these answers. If you're like me, you like answers that make you feel light and fluffy inside, but most of these answers tend to be heavier than that. They weigh me down. They're hard to carry.

Part of my frustration is with Jesus. As valuable as it is to observe his life and read his words, he answered relatively few questions about my life's big issues. I've mentioned how he often answers a question with a question; sometimes he even answers with a riddle, a story, or some ambiguous anecdote. It didn't take long to realize my life had an array of uncertainty that Jesus didn't specifically deal with.

As much as I feel entitled to a life of ease, comfort, and absolute moral clarity, these answers didn't provide that at all. Instead of a black-and-white yes or no, most of these answers make me feel like I'm still living in the gray, trying to decide which gray area is better, or at least less destructive. And I hate that.

But maybe that's what it's all about. The searching. The discovering. The grasping. The learning.

Anyway, here's my attempt at some answers. And who knows? Maybe I even got some of them right.

Why would a loving God let bad things happen to good people?

A lot has been written about this because it's big. I'll hit the ground running with this one. It's one of the Big Three, as I like to say—one of the top three unanswered questions (I'll get to the other two) that cause many people to stay away or walk away from God.

It's often expressed in other ways, like, "Why is there so much suffering and evil in the world?" I've asked it myself on more than one occasion. And though I've formulated an answer, I still ask.

The ability to ask it is, in itself, a representation of the answer. But I think the pain prevents me from seeing this.

Pain is difficult to ignore. Something about pain demands an answer, an assignment of blame. It just doesn't make sense that bad things should happen to good people. When they do, we inevitably blame God. Who else is there to blame?

But that may not be quite fair. There may be others responsible.

Think about choices, especially when it comes to love. I once bought my wife a teddy bear that said, "I love you!" when she squeezed it. As cute as it was, there was nothing special about that because the bear had no choice in the matter.

When someone chooses to love us, it brings healing to our hearts. I think this is something we share with God. Not that God needs healing, but this innate desire in us to love and be loved is put there by God. In his brilliance and in an expression of true love, he gave humans the ability to love as he does—to *choose* to love.

In contrast, God would never demean humanity by not giving us the capacity to choose. Choice is wonderful—when we choose to love. But choice is hideous—when we choose to hate.

The problem with evil is really a problem with our ability to choose. That's where the real blame goes. People choose to do evil things, and that always creates negative consequences. I suppose we're all villains to some degree, because we all make wrong choices and do bad things. Everyone's guilty.

Some say this is God's fault because he gave us the ability to choose. But I feel a little juvenile saying that. Looking at it more maturely, we can't escape the realization that evil is the responsibility of those who choose it. And if we hate evil, the best we can do is become more responsible with our capacity to choose and try to influence others in theirs.

Choice is a risk. Coupled with other aspects of our nature, it can be reckless and destructive. Once I understand good and evil, love and hate, I discover who's to blame.

So the answer is this: bad things happen because some people choose to do bad things.

Why did God let this happen to me?

We've all asked this. I asked it when we lost our first child.

This question comes when life is just hard and not necessarily because of the consequences of others' choices. Like when you are diagnosed with cancer.

Or it doesn't have to be so heavy. Maybe it's when the jerk at work gets the promotion you wanted. Or the baby won't stop crying all night.

This question really picks up where the last one leaves off. We're in awful circumstances for reasons outside our control, and apparently due to no one's wrong choices. We're the recipients of misfortune, for no apparent reason. Sometimes life is random and painful.

But again, we look for blame.

The answers start with admitting the obvious. This world, this existence, is broken. It isn't functioning the way it should. That much we can all agree on.

God never wanted us to experience pain or sorrow or tears or even death. Maybe that's why we get so mad when it happens. It's as if we think we're entitled to the perfect life. Actually, we're right. God wants us to have that feeling we experience on vacation or on our honeymoon—that carefree, stress-free, timeless bubble, away from all the cares. We don't care what we eat, where we go, when we get there, or how much it costs. We don't read the newspaper or care about getting to bed on time so we'll have the energy for tomorrow's responsibilities.

But, eventually, we have to get back to reality.

The thing is, we *are* entitled to the perfect life—just not in *this* life. That's in the next life, in heaven. In the next reality. For now, things are broken.

Ultimately, this is also a result of human choices, but not specifically our own. When humanity originally chose, in one fateful action, to disobey God (the first sin), something broke. It broke badly. And it's still broken.

I'm referring, of course, to Adam and Eve. The introduction of sin, or evil, caused the world as God made it to shatter. Maybe we don't all believe in the literal story of Adam and Eve, but the essence is true nonetheless. Evil has, for the time being, become part of the DNA of our existence. It breaks things and causes pain. A lot of pain.

But can't God stop the pain from happening in certain circumstances? The answer, of course, is yes. In fact, I'm of the opinion that he stops the pain much more than we realize. He just doesn't do it all the time, and even when he does, we often don't recognize it. If we did, we wouldn't ask this question as much, or maybe not at all.

After all these generations of brokenness, the good news is that healing will come one day. God is simply waiting, for reasons of his own (another question altogether), to make it happen.

I recognize this answer might not satisfy your intellect. That's okay. These situations don't appeal to our intellects. If they did, we would simply rationalize away the pain and concede that there's a random element to life that has no particular rhyme or reason. But these situations pull on our emotions.

Every pain and illness, and all the general brokenness we experience in this life, will one day be fixed and healed. That's a promise from God.[32] But there's no guarantee it will happen in our lifetimes. It may not be fulfilled until the afterlife.

For now, the world is broken. That's why.

How do you explain dinosaurs?

Let's lighten the mood for a moment.

Dinosaurs were real. The Bible seems to indicate them in different ways. Depending on the translation, the Bible uses terms like *leviathan, dragon,* and *behemoth* to describe large mysterious beasts.[33]

Many scholars speculate that after the catastrophic flood in Noah's day, the environment changed so drastically that the dinosaurs couldn't survive. Climates, oxygen levels, humidity levels, and sun exposure all contributed to their demise.[34]

Speaking of the flood, how could all those animals fit in Noah's ark?

This one's fun and actually pretty easy when you apply some basic arithmetic, architecture, and science.[35] I'm not going to lie though—you still have to accept the supernatural in order to believe this was even possible.

First, let's talk about how big the ark was. Based on the dimensions given in the Bible,[36] and converting them to modern terms we're familiar with, the ark was about as long as one and a half football fields (450 feet), as wide as four Chevrolet Suburban SUV's lined end to end (75 feet), and more than four stories tall (45 feet). That means it was approximately 1.5 million cubic feet in size, and it looked kind of like a humongous coffin.

Assuming that about half this space was taken up for infrastructure and storage, that leaves 750,000 cubic feet for the animals. That's big enough for about 125,000 animals the size of sheep.

Assuming that only 15 to 20 percent of the animals were larger than that (a fair assessment based on species alive today), there would be room for about 50,000 animals, along with Noah's family and even some hired hands, plus everything needed to sustain them all, with room to spare.

It's also important to note how animal species have evolved since then within their own kind. For example, today there are over four hundred types of dogs, but they all came from a dozen or so distinct species. Keeping this in mind for all the animal kingdom, there would need to be only some 16,000 unique animal species on the ark to account for all the variations we've seen in the animal kingdom from then until today.

So all the animals and supplies could feasibly (and easily) fit in the ark. Now, the smell is another subject altogether.

Why can't Christians agree?

I don't know why. I wish they could. They would surely be a greater force for good.

The best way I can approach this question is through lasagna.

I love lasagna, but not every helping of lasagna I've ever had. Some are too cheesy. Some use the wrong cheeses. Some are too meaty. Some have veggies with the meat. Some don't even have meat, if you can believe that. Everyone has a different recipe.

Just as every batch of lasagna is different, every Christian understands faith differently. People have different backgrounds, tastes, temperaments, family traditions, personalities, etc. Combined with our ability to choose, we create our own recipes for faith. It can be messy, ugly, or dangerous, but it's just the way things are.

As worthwhile as it would be if they did, I don't think Christians will ever completely agree. They never did. Jesus was always mediating among the disciples when they fought. In some ways, this is bad, but in other ways, we benefit from it.

I'm grateful for those times in the past when some Christians broke free from negative directions that others were taking because they saw things differently (mass printing of the Bible centuries ago and the Protestant Reformation, for example). Not to mention, we have almost the whole New Testament because of differences that needed to be resolved.

I know I've used a simplified illustration here to describe an ugly reality. Maybe Christians should value their representation of Christ so much that no one could ever compare them to lasagna. Something we can all keep in mind.

Are homosexuals born gay?

This is the second of the Big Three, and it's a question Christians tend to spend a lot of time and effort on. Christians who focus on this issue are branded as intolerant, often rightly so. There's no arguing—this is a hot-button topic.

The question and its answer aren't as important as the underlying issues. But first let's answer the question.

Yes, in my opinion, people can be born gay. I'm no scientist, but I have some experience counseling people. From what I can tell of the human experience, everyone's born with certain raw materials with regard to personality and temperament. This combines with early formative environments to help shape the people we become. So why couldn't people be born with natural tendencies toward that particular sexual orientation? This is who they are.

I've had friends and acquaintances over the years that were homosexual. I never asked them specifically if they chose that lifestyle or if they thought they were born gay. It never mattered to me. But I'm sure, from what they've experienced, they wouldn't choose the lifestyle. Who would want to live with all the baggage that comes with it? They probably would also tell you that their sexuality was something they felt naturally. I can accept that.

But let's talk about what's really important—the underlying issues that fuel this conflict.

The first is tolerance. It's a difficult virtue to live out. In fact, in the name of tolerance, people actually tell others they have to agree with them and their values. That's intolerance. Both sides of this issue are guilty here.

Individuals caught up in this conflict may never agree, and I think that's okay. The solution is to find commonality. Conflicts like this can be diffused when both sides sincerely agree on what they have in common and take measures to promote and protect that. That's true tolerance. We just need to treat others the way we want to be treated (remember the golden rule?). We also need to remember we're all different. God designed us that way. He also designed us to be responsible for what we do with those differences. So, we need to agree to respect each other.

Respect is even better than tolerance. After all, who wants to be merely tolerated? It's demeaning. Through respect we can learn to do the better thing and accept others, regardless of differences.

The second issue is morality. It's homosexual behavior that Christians tend to have a problem with, not the person or his or her orientation. You may have heard the statement, "Hate the sin, but not the sinner." I hate that phrase. Who really feels valued and respected when approached that way? Besides, I don't think this is actually possible for people who approach the situation like this. Who can really separate the two? Most people tend to hate both, even when they say those words. So I think Christians need to stop saying things like this. It's condescending.

Besides, we're all sinners in different ways, so Christians should probably be hating their own sin as much as anyone else's. None of us is perfect. I seem to remember a story of Jesus saying whoever is without sin to throw the first stone. That's not to say we won't ever evaluate someone else's life or actions. But let it be when we are asked or when there is a relationship to build on.

I also think each side of this issue tries to force its morality on the other. But morality is based on beliefs and values, which are unique to each individual and thus cannot, and should not, be forced.

Beliefs are interesting things. Many times people that believe something passionately will view it as their duty to get others to believe it. But we can't always get others to think like we do, and that's okay.

Mutual respect is the answer again. But too often, neither side wants to give in first. So they pout with arms folded waiting like third-graders for the other person to say they're sorry first.

Sincere beliefs should inspire you to live in a way that's so authentic it compels others to be curious about what you believe. It's lifestyle that convinces, not arguments.

Again, Jesus is the supreme example of this. People like Martin Luther King Jr. and Gandhi all challenged and changed core values and beliefs in others through this type of approach.

The challenge is to learn to hold authentic beliefs *and* respect the beliefs of others at the same time. It's not easy. We have to learn to accept those who don't agree philosophically with our lifestyles and decisions. It doesn't necessarily mean we agree with what they believe. It just means we're accepting them.

I have some family members who don't like how my wife and I live. We have such a different worldview and life philosophy that it simply rubs them wrong. This isn't to say we're overt, overbearing, or disrespectful toward any of them. We simply are who we are, and that's contrary enough. We get along most of the time, and we see each other and spend time together. We respectfully agree to disagree and move on. Except for the normal family feuding, we accept our differences without stirring up hatred.

The simple solution to the complex issue of how to approach homosexuality is the same as it ever was. It's to learn to accept others without necessarily approving. Just like we want to be accepted.

I know I've left unanswered the question of whether I believe homosexuality is wrong. Let me say instead that I believe in Jesus and the Bible, and I also believe God views all sin the same, "because all people are the same: everyone has sinned and fallen short of God's glorious standard."[37] I have my own set of problems. I eat too much; I'm greedy, selfish, and envious, all of which are sins.[38] Do you still love and respect me?

So, are people born gay? Who cares? Everybody has his or her own issues to deal with.

Is Christianity the only way?

This is the last of the Big Three—and probably *the* big one.

There's no way for me to communicate what I believe about this issue without offending someone. But here is my best effort.

Christianity claims that it's the only path to God. Can that be true?

Let's talk again about belief. In a general sense, if people truly believe something to their cores, it will separate them from those who don't believe the same thing. I'm not saying people should go out of their way to alienate others because of their beliefs. But passionately held beliefs will be polarizing to some degree.

Christianity is no exception.

We all know the popular Jesus—the one who said so many generous, patient, tolerant, and graceful things. Everyone loves the popular Jesus. Everyone likes to quote him in speeches to support personal causes. At Easter and Christmas, the popular Jesus helps sell merchandise and fill churches. Many forward-thinking people quote the popular Jesus to resolve problems. World leaders tackle current events relying on the words of the popular Jesus.

But that's not who I'm talking about.

The unpopular Jesus is not that marketable. Some of his statements are blunt and tactless. These aren't quoted much.

Here's one of them: *"I am the way, and the truth, and the life. The only way to the Father is through me."*[39] He also said, *"I tell you the truth, whoever hears my word and believes him who sent me has eternal life and will not be condemned; he has crossed over from death to life."*[40] And this: *"I am the resurrection and the life. He who believes in me will live, even though he dies; and whoever lives and believes in me will never die."*[41]

Clearly, Jesus needs to brush up on his marketing techniques. Some people don't even know Jesus said things like that.

Many people don't understand that Jesus came to call people to a decision, because *God* calls people to a decision. Jesus wanted to communicate in word and action how much God loved them, so they would choose to love God.

Anyone who's interested in spiritual matters must decide if he believes these words of the unpopular Jesus, and if he'll accept them.

I have another question: Does God, through Jesus, *require*

exclusivity? And is that even fair?

For some reason, I have a problem with allowing God the right of exclusivity. If God doesn't allow each individual to discover his or her own way to the afterlife, I call him cruel. I even say he isn't transcendent, or any kind of God who's worth loving, especially if the resulting consequence is an eternity absent from his presence (hell, if you will).

But does that really make sense? After all, I practice exclusivity in my own life. And others expect it from me. If I told my wife on our wedding night that she would have to let me share love sexually with others for the sake of love itself, our marriage probably wouldn't work. I might try to convince her that the more love we share with others, the more love we will contribute to the world. I could love my wife, the neighbor lady, *and* the woman in the grocery store and whoever else was willing to share. This communal love would bring more good, and the universe would become a better place as we added and added and added, right? She would probably call me a pig and send me packing—appropriately so. She wants exclusivity in our relationship. She wants fidelity. That is, if I truly love her.

So I think my problem with the idea that God would require exclusivity is actually something else. It's a problem with a relational expectation I don't think God should have.

Nevertheless, I've come to see that God, in his faithful love for us, doesn't want us to devote ourselves to whatever "god" on the smorgasbord tickles our fancy. So I settle on a connection with God being relational in nature, and, therefore, exclusive in practice—in a healthy, authentic way.

I have to ask myself whether I'll accept such a nonnegotiable relational expectation from God. Will I allow him to require loyalty and faithfulness? If so, I have to allow him to define that loyalty as he sees fit.

I think it's fair to let God require exclusivity in the relationship. And I don't think it's about a monopoly on belief, religion, or belief systems. It's about God wanting a relationship with us and wanting us to spend eternity with him. Certainly, any of us is free not to establish that relationship.

Discussing this issue of exclusivity often prompts people to ask more questions: *What about the people that had no opportunity to hear about God or Jesus? What if they grew up in a different part of the world under a different belief system? What if they never met a true Christian or saw a correct representation of Jesus and his teachings in action, but instead saw only fakes and hypocrites? How could Christianity be the "only way" for them when they never knew enough about it to really understand?*

These are valid questions, and I don't know the answers. I do know this: God can figure this stuff out himself. I believe he's perfectly fair, so I trust him to decide. As for me, I have heard about Jesus and his difficult sayings and his calls to choose, so I'm responsible. Will I rationalize those issues away because I won't allow God to require relational exclusivity? Will I deny him because others have misrepresented him?

So, *is* Christianity the only way?

Each of us has to answer that individually. Personally, I find comfort in those hard-to-accept words I quoted from Jesus. At least he left no doubt about his answer to the question of how to spend eternity with him.

× × × ×

And if I haven't answered a question and you really, really need
an answer, just insert *because I said so* or *that's just the way it is*.
Just kidding. Either way, ask your questions. But be willing to listen
for the answers no matter how uncomfortable they may be.

#9 Church

My friend Jorge can eat whatever he wants whenever he wants, and he stays skinny. I hate him. I'm not like that. I haven't seen my belt since I was eighteen, and I haven't seen my shoes for about ten years.

Like most people, I've gone through spurts of dieting, but it never seems to last.

First the Atkins Diet. I really liked that one because I could eat all the bacon and steak I wanted. By the way, is there anything bacon doesn't improve? Burgers, green beans, eggs, baked potatoes—bacon makes them all taste better. Anyway, I eventually fell off the Atkins wagon. I couldn't stay away from bread, pasta, and potatoes. Sometimes there's just nothing better than a big plate of spaghetti with garlic bread. The Atkins Diet became the Fatkins Diet, as I gained back all the weight.

Then Body for Life was the rage for a while. On that one, I ate healthier, as well as more often. The idea was to break down three meals a day into six smaller ones, speeding up my metabolism to keep it working around the clock. To make it effective, you had to stay on this frequent-meal schedule. This was great, since I love to eat.

I worked in an office at the time, and there always seemed to be food on my desk. In a meeting, I'd bring out my sandwich. On the phone, I'd start chomping on carrot sticks. Unfortunately, this can come off as rude. It also became inconvenient. It wasn't long before Body for Life became Fatty for Life.

The last one I tried was the South Beach Diet. That was good because I could eat carbs in moderation, except for sweets, since they're bad carbs. I didn't mind, because I don't really crave sweets. But the hard part was not drinking soda, as you may have guessed. So, the South Beach Diet became the Mouth Beach Dict, and I gained it all back.

Along with dieting should come exercise. But I hate exercise. There's a freakish minority that loves going to the gym daily, but I dread physical workouts—though I always feel good after the fact.

That's how I am. There's something in me—and in all of us—that knows it's important to eat right and do regular physical activity. I don't hate being healthy; I just hate all the work it takes to get there and stay there.

I hate even more all the work it takes to be spiritually healthy—which explains my feeling about church. Over the years, I've hated church like I hate diet and exercise. Something inside me wants to stay away from church—while at the same time, something inside me wants to go. I know I can't just sit around and expect to become spiritually healthy.

It takes action.

Church, Inc.

You've probably set foot in a church at some point in your life, be it Easter or Christmas, or a friend invited you. Afterward, one of two things happened: Something unexplainable appealed to you and you decided to go back; or, more likely, it didn't pique your curiosity and you never returned.

There was a reason the church you visited was like it was. Whether you realized it or not, that church fit into one of the following descriptions: traditional, contemporary, charismatic, Pentecostal, evangelical, postmodern, purpose-driven, seeker-sensitive, emergent, emerging, missional—there are more, but that's enough for my purpose. The thing is, none of that probably mattered to you. You may not even have known all those existed, let alone what they meant.

What probably *did* matter to you was whether you felt welcomed by the people there and could understand what the pastor or preacher or priest or bishop was saying. At least that's how I felt, thinking back to churches I've visited over the years. Those were the reasons I either did or didn't go back.

What's funny is that even though we have boring or even bad experiences at church, many of us still go back. Why do we do that, if it isn't that great? We could simply stay home and talk about Easter or Christmas with our families around the table.

Why do we return? I think, for the most part, it's because something inside us tells us it's a good place to be. Like diet and exercise, it provides something we know, deep down, we need. No pill or quick fix can bring spiritual fitness. It needs regular attention.

I'm convinced most human beings are innately curious about spiritual things. We recognize there's a spiritual element to life that can't necessarily be explained; yet, it's there nonetheless. We can even be drawn to it unknowingly.

After all, being part of a playoff baseball game in a stadium full of people is a spiritual experience of sorts. That's how I felt when the Red Sox finally won the World Series in 2004. I'm not even their fan, but I was rooting for them with my friend Bob, who's diehard, and who told me they hadn't won it since 1918. I was moved to my core with the rest of the fans when their team finally broke the "Curse of the Bambino."

Getting a sneak peak at a highly anticipated movie in a packed theater can also be a spiritual experience. In 1997, when my wife and I were dating, we got tickets to a preview showing of *Titanic*. It was intense, and the theater was silent the entire three hours. We all walked out quiet and somber. Without a doubt, it was spiritual like no other movie, which is why it's still the highest grossing release of all time.

Watching your favorite band at a sold-out show can be a spiritual experience too. It was for me when I saw U2 on their *Joshua Tree* tour at the Orange Bowl in Miami back in 1987. It was amazing. It took hours for the stadium to empty out because no one wanted to leave. We were moved deep down and didn't want it to end.

Most people are interested in spiritual things on some level and curious to understand them more. And many of us recognize that church at least *should be* a nexus and catalyst for spiritual matters.

Just as joining a gym keeps us accountable in our health, church can keep us in check spiritually. It can help us attain healing and wholeness deep down. It seems to function much like a combination spiritual gym and hospital. It challenges and trains us to grow beyond who we are, so we can be better equipped to go out and meet the world each day. Doing life can be draining, so we need help in refueling. Doing life can be confusing, so getting a little guidance doesn't hurt either.

That's why I think church continues to play some part in our lives. Certainly, you don't have to go to church to be spiritual. But it's hard for me to separate regular church attendance from my spiritual health over the years.

Still, I've been given many reasons to question church. I've wondered what good it is and why it even exists. Sadly, there are things I've learned at church that aren't spiritual in the least. I hate these things, and I think you may too. They're the main reasons I've avoided church at times.

And they're why many of us don't go back.

St. Stale Assembly

When I was nine or ten, I went to a church in an old, beautiful building filled with statues, stained glass murals, and paintings. We sat toward the front in a well-crafted wooden pew. Though the place was half-filled with people, it was very quiet. I guess that's because every little sound echoed like crazy.

The church service lasted a little over an hour, but seemed longer. Old hymns were sung, accompanied by a giant organ that took up the entire back wall and seemed a little too loud, probably because of the echo. We also stood up a bunch of times to repeat things together. Some were in a book, and some were things everyone else had memorized. I couldn't keep up, so I felt like an outsider.

Eventually, the main guy, wearing a robe, stood up and talked. His message didn't really make sense to me. He spoke like he was very important and he used big words. I don't remember him reading from a Bible or talking about it. Luckily, his talk was only about twenty minutes.

Eventually, to my relief, the whole thing was over. It was one of the most boring and sterile experiences of my life. And all the while, no one there spoke to us, not even to say hello.

Indirectly, this church taught me that spiritual things can bore you to death and aren't worth trying to learn. I even remember thinking God might not be real. Or maybe he was just as bored there as I was.

That old church needed to be renamed something like St. Stale and Stagnant of the Blessed and Bored. It was death to my early spiritual curiosities. It felt "holy," but empty at the same time. It was beautiful and grand, but full of ritual and pretense.

I'll shut up about it and end this description in the same way they ended the church service. Ready? Imagine it real loud and echoing, as everyone says it together: *AHHHHMEN!*

First Church of the Spirits Without the Alcohol

My next church experience wasn't until I was a teenager, when a friend invited me. This one definitely wasn't boring. In fact, it was really exciting, maybe even a little frightful.

The building wasn't quite as grand as St. Stale. It had simple stained glass windows in solid colors. The inside looked like a nice auditorium.

As we walked in, music was playing in the background and the place was nearly full. Everyone was friendly. I was greeted and welcomed dozens of times.

BOOM!

The service started with music — *loud* music. The band had every instrument you would expect to see at a live rock concert. And lots of singers. As things progressed, there were solos of all kinds: guitar, bass guitar, vocal, piano/keyboard, and drum. The noise and energy levels kept building.

Everyone seemed excited to be there, maybe a little too excited for my taste. Some were standing and singing with their hands in the air as if reaching for something. Some marched in place to the music, and others were dancing freestyle in the aisles.

At different points during the songs, each band member seemed to go off in his own direction musically. It sounded like bad fusion-style jazz (which I hate). Everyone got a turn, and I thought that was confusing.

Then it all got weirder.

These musical freestyle moments seemed to prompt the crowd to do its own personal vocal fusion. Everyone did something different—chants, moans, all types of "singing." Some people were saying what sounded to me like repetitious gibberish— "shundu-lah, shundulah, shundulah," or "my-momma-bought-a-new-Honda, my-momma-bought-a-new-Honda." I was uncomfortable. Was this a church or a drug trance? (Only later, in the car with my friend, did

I learn this was called "speaking in tongues.")

Finally, after long, drawn-out prayers, the main guy—wearing a suit—stepped up to the fancy podium ("pulpit" he called it several times, as if it represented some type of authority). He prayed before he preached. And preached and preached and preached. He went long and hard. He also got very sweaty, probably from swinging around his giant burgundy, leather-bound Bible.

I give him credit. He believed what he was saying, and he was excited about it. He spoke for over an hour, and the people in the crowd seemed to be genuinely tuned in. He talked a lot about Jesus and referred to his Bible repeatedly. Initially this seemed good. But at times he got so passionate that he yelled, and I started feeling like I was being hammered—like Saddam Hussein in the '90s during Desert Storm when they played Guns N' Roses at sonic levels to drive him out.

I thought his talk would never end, and I wondered why everything in this church was so loud. It's good to be excited and all, but weren't they worried about it looking like a circus show?

Then it got even weirder. After the preaching came the closing songs. Again, it built up to musical and personal fusion, including the chanting, moaning, etc. To this point, I'd been relatively patient with the whole scene, but I *really* disliked what happened next. The people in the crowd were directed to put their hands on the visitors and to "pray over" them. Yeah, gotta love that.

I had about a half dozen people around me with their hands on my shoulders and back. An older lady leaned in and told me, in a kind voice, to try to "speak in tongues." (As I mentioned, I didn't learn what this meant until later.) I was confused and uncomfortable.

I pretended to try, just so she'd leave me alone.

Then a man commanded any demons that might be in me to come out. The people surrounding me gave me several little nudges, I guess to help push out the demons and send them on their way.

The whole service lasted almost three hours.

Funny thing is, I endured this church experience several more times over the next few months, because the person inviting me was a good friend. Each time I was confused and uncomfortable, and I eventually stopped going. It was just a little too weird for me. While there I didn't feel like God was dead, and I definitely wasn't bored, but it didn't give me a deep sense of spiritual clarity. I always went home emotionally charged, but not really remembering anything of substance I could apply to real life. And I certainly couldn't imagine bringing one of my other friends there.

I haven't been back to a church like that since.

United Capital Chapel

A few years later, I went to a church service that started out in an unremarkable way—music by a band, then teaching by the main guy—but then it transitioned into something unforgettable.

A team of about a dozen guys with bulging muscles came out dressed in matching spandex outfits (this was the late '80s). The stage was filled with barbells and other props for the show. Pulsating, loud music exploded, and it all began. I guess I would describe it as a strong man contest meets a karate competition meets the circus meets church.

The spandex guys took turns proving their manhood. There were great feats of strength and lots of grunting and yelling. There was the typical board breaking with kicks and karate chops. One guy even broke a baseball bat barehanded. Another one ripped a phone book in half. Another ran through a wall of ice, which was pretty cool (*ha!*). He got scratched up a little and was bleeding.

One of the better feats was a guy breaking a stack of bricks with his forehead. I always love that one. If you're like me, you secretly hope those guys knock themselves out while leaving the bricks intact. *That's what you get for trying a stunt like that!* At least that's what I picture their moms and dads telling them as kids when they attempted such things, since I'm sure their best ideas came from their childhoods. But, why were they doing these things as adults in a church service? (To be fair, I did learn that this was a special event and not what they normally did at this church.)

The strangest strength display came at the end. The main strong guy—whose wrists were wrapped in duct tape—had a police officer come out on stage and place official police-issue handcuffs on him. The cop was there to verify they were real, because the muscle man promised to attempt to break out of them. Are your eyes rolling? Mine were.

Mr. Wrist-wrap explained that the duct tape was for protection. The night before, this stunt had sent him to the ER; he'd cut the veins in his wrists while trying to break free. (Are your eyes rolling now?) But he promised he wouldn't let that stop him. Obviously, it was all a lie, and I was sure God didn't like lying, especially in church.

Anyway, the showmanship ensued as he seemingly struggled to escape. He grunted and strained, paused, yelled, and strained some more, apparently utilizing all his strength to no avail. Dramatically, he gave up after several minutes.

At this point, he assured us he couldn't do it alone. He needed us all to pray for God to give him supernatural strength, like Samson in the Bible.

The showmanship continued. He strained and yelled, "Pray! *Pray!*" Then, "Pray *harder!*" And then, *"Pray LOUDER!"* After several minutes of this, he broke the handcuffs with the last ounce of his strength (of course!). The crowd hollered in relief and roared in celebration.

That's when the showmanship gave way to salesmanship.

All this buildup was to make way for the pitch. Once the tension was released with the handcuff-breaking display, the strong guy started to talk about God and Jesus. He was pretty good, and I got what he was saying. He was well spoken and passionate, but I just couldn't get past the whole duct tape/ER lie.

The climax of his talk really turned me off. He hit up everyone in the crowd for money, and he hit 'em hard. It was tasteless, especially since a show like this attracts young kids (who don't have any money) and many people who don't normally go to church. Shamelessly, he went on and on, saying it took a considerable budget to fund this ministry, especially since they took their families with them when they traveled. That left me wondering. I can understand that when you travel for a living you might bring your family occasionally. But why all the time? I'm no financial expert, but stopping this practice would probably cut their expenses at least in half.

At one point he looked at a woman in the front row and prompted her, "Honey, get out that checkbook. Don't worry if that's your last hundred dollars. God will bless you for giving it!" That was just plain pathetic. I couldn't believe God was behind tactics like this.

Honestly, I think the whole show idea wasn't all bad. I get it. There were a lot of families in the crowd with their kids and they loved it. It was professionally done. I just didn't like the lying and money-grubbing at the end. It gave me the impression heaven was about to be foreclosed on and the saints thrown out in the streets. Was God broke? Did Jesus need to get a second job to help cover the bills? I remember thinking, *If God's always on the verge of going under, how can he be responsible with my spirituality?*

I wasn't interested in a church that would present spiritual things in this manner. I understand money is a part of life and things cost money, but it seems like churches and ministries shouldn't seem so irresponsible or greedy when representing God—which is what it's all about, isn't it?

I never went back to that church.

The Perfect Enough Community Church

My guess is that most people who visit a church have one of those three experiences I had, in some way, shape, or form. That's one of the main reasons they don't return.

I know there's no perfect church. Well, that's not exactly true. I once drove by one. I'm not kidding. I was lost and driving in circles trying to find my way to the baseball game with a friend when we drove by "The Perfect Church"—that was the name on their sign. I almost crashed doing a double take, then stopped for a picture. I guess I could never go there; I'd be afraid of ruining it.

A few months later, I drove by a church that had the phrase "Christians Meet Here" in large letters right under the church's name. But what about people who aren't Christians? Doesn't God care about them? Where are they supposed to go to search out spiritual matters?

Then there's the church I drive by several times a week on my way home. On the sign out front it says, "Welcome," but on weekdays the entrance is barricaded. Seems to send a mixed signal.

It doesn't take physical barricades to keep most people away. They avoid church for other reasons. Some say they don't like church because it's full of hypocrites and fake people. I understand. I said that, too, until I realized I wasn't so perfect myself. In fact, I've never met anyone who is.

I'm glad church is filled with hypocrites. That means they have room for another one like me. Where else can we go to become better people and grow spiritually? Isn't church really *the* place for hypocrites? I go to church to change me, not change the church. Besides, my favorite restaurants and movie theaters are filled with hypocrites too, but I still go there.

Someone once told me he didn't go to church because he wasn't into "organized religion." I liked the sound of that. We talked about how "the man" is always trying to bring us down, as we equated church with the evils of corporate greed and big oil. It sounded so intellectual. But was there some hidden agenda? And what's the alternative to organized religion? How appealing does "disorganized religion" sound? So all this broke down as I thought it through.

Eventually, I admitted to myself I was trying to avoid church for personal reasons, like I did with exercise. I didn't want to be challenged. I wanted to go on being spiritually lazy.

I know there's no perfect church. But I don't need a perfect church. I just need one that's perfect enough.

I wish the average church visit were a little different. I don't have all the answers, but I have some ideas.

On a basic level, I think a church's environment needs to be accepting and the communication needs to be helpful. When I walk in, it would be good if I felt welcome right away, and everyone's sincerely friendly. Not too close, and no long awkward moments of direct eye contact. Just a simple "Hello" or "Welcome" with a smile is good.

The music should be a lot like what's on the radio, since that's what most people listen to anyway. I once read that hymns were originally written to old bar tunes so people would feel welcome when they went to church. I like that principle.

I also think the people playing the music and singing should be relatively good at it. I've heard some real crappy performances in my church visits. Just because people love God, or are related to the pastor, doesn't make them good singers or talented musicians. They don't have to be rock star-caliber. They just can't be *American Idol* rejects still trying to make a go of it for God.

The teaching should be understandable. In this day and age, applying spiritual principles from an ancient book (the Bible) can be confusing. So learning something that's helpful and practical, maybe even plain and simple, is good—since I'm plagued by a mild case of adult ADHD. Truth be told, I even want to feel a little entertained at church, to keep my short attention span engaged. After all, I watch TV shows all the time that present problems and find life-changing solutions, all in thirty minutes (including ten minutes for commercials that, incidentally, do the same thing in thirty seconds).

So a little entertainment is good. It may not sound very spiritual of me to say, but it's true nonetheless.

In the end, I want to leave church feeling somewhat equipped to live my life in a way that makes a difference. This will help me not forget what I heard by the time I go to lunch. I want to feel inspired to be a better person and assured I can do it. I want to be challenged in a way that isn't dogmatic or judgmental, maybe stressing the benefits, possibilities, and obvious consequences. This would probably make me more willing to change.

If money comes up, which I'm fine with, let it somehow be geared toward the people who go to that church regularly. That would help visitors feel a little more comfortable, especially since regular attendees should be the ones supporting the church.

And since I have kids, I want them to quickly feel comfortable there. Kids can be a little reserved when it comes to new places. So, friendly people and an energetic environment would be good. I would want them to have fun and learn something too. It would be amazing if a children's program at a church could be kind of like Nickelodeon meets Disney, but with an important spiritual message instead of SpongeBob looking for his lost booger. And these principles should be adapted and applied to different age levels (pre-K, elementary, teens).

I also want to know that my kids are safe. That might even be more important than them having fun. Knowing that my kids are never alone with an adult and that all the people working with the kids have had thorough background checks would help me feel comfortable as a parent. If this weren't the case, I definitely would be hesitant to go back.

It would also be great for newcomers to be able to connect with other people other than during the Sunday morning hustle and bustle of getting their families in and out of church. This would go a long way to helping new people feel more comfortable and "at home."

I know all these things sound obvious, but I don't think they are—which might explain why the average church in America has only seventy members. Church attendance is decreasing while the population is increasing. In addition, most churches experience 80 percent turnover every two years. These are discouraging facts. Obviously, many people feel like church is irrelevant and don't go back.

Good churches are rare, but there are some. I go to one. It's a place to learn about life, love, hope, and purpose. Where can people go for these things if the church isn't there for them?

Spiritual Health and Life Change Center

Ever since I was a young adult, I've been going to different churches and volunteering in various ministries, because I was captivated by their compassion and devotion. Sure, sometimes it contributed to my disillusionment and hate, but it was also pivotal in my growth.

I believe in the local church. I believe it's the hope of every community. I believe in the church so much that I even helped start one in Miami. We started with about seven people, and five years later, there were almost four hundred. It was amazing. I eventually became an assistant pastor and in time got to be involved in nearly every aspect of the ministry. It was one of the most important things I've ever done. I even got to teach several times. Those were some of the best years of my life and also some of the hardest.

I once had someone ask me what those of us who worked at the church did Monday through Friday. He thought we sat around praying and reading the Bible all day. Nothing could be further from the truth.

People constantly came for guidance, though many didn't want to be told what to do. I suppose there's a little rebellious teenager in everyone. We saw careers, marriages, and families being ruined by destructive behaviors. We spent countless hours listening and helping people change. But sometimes they would ruin everything with one stupid decision.

The church was really more like a spiritual hospital than a gym. Actually, like an ER. People often came to church as a last resort. They put off their own well being until they were flat lining. When there was nowhere else to turn for help, for comfort, for support, or direction on how to clean up the mess, they would show up at church. Which is great. That's what church is for. But why wait until things get so bad?

Ministry was draining, but also rewarding. I was there when families started and when wrecked marriages were restored. I saw drug addictions beaten and abuse overcome. I also watched when families buried parents, or worse, their only child.

We believed that a church should bear witness to the fact that God and Jesus are real and alive. This very truth should be reflected in everything from signage to sermons, from main entrance to music arrangements, from what the kids do to the basic core values. Everything was to be done with excellence.

We worked hard and often around the clock. We prayed for energy every day. And every week we asked ourselves what we could do better.

I lost a lot of sleep. Sometimes it was hard to relax on days off because I thought I might be missing someone who needed help. Several years later, I'm still dealing with some of the burnout.

These are the challenges of every church. So, I have the utmost respect for people who do ministry like that and stick with it.

I also think these people have to regularly look from the outside in and ask why their churches exist. What is its purpose? Every church has a mission and strategy. It may or may not be intentional, but a strategy exists nonetheless. They're creating models by how they do what they do and the environments they create. Sometimes you can even see it simply by driving by.

There's nothing better than finding a good church with the right strategy. It's the place where people can learn how to be better people—better friends, better employees, better fathers, better mothers, better husbands, better wives, better neighbors, better citizens. Because anything that isn't growing and changing is stagnating, like water pooling at the edge of the driveway. People are no different.

Honestly, churches are pretty much the only places teaching these things. Churches are the ones starting soup kitchens, sending relief to the poor, and helping people put their lives back together. I remember a church in South Florida helping all the residents of an apartment building that burned down. They replaced all their belongings and even gave them money to get through the whole process. If there were no churches, who would do this stuff? Sure, federal and local governments can help, but that's not enough. And how effective are they really? It's not personal enough. We need good churches in every community. They invest so much when they're filled with people committed to change and growth.

If we don't go to church, where will we be inspired to do good and become better people? How will we have personal accountability with regard to our characters? How will we get strength from being around people with the same goals? Remember, we're relational beings and we need each other. And church is a good thing.

I go to church regularly these days. But, like exercising, I don't always want to. Sunday mornings are always a struggle. I wake up, and the last thing I want to do after working all week and doing a bunch of chores and errands on Saturday is get the entire house all in a frenzy as we feed and dress the kids and rush off to church. Plus, my wife and I always manage to get into a fight. We also run late, which we never do for anything else.

There's that moment when I think how much more productive it would be to just sip coffee and read the paper or watch that Star Trek marathon or go out for a leisurely breakfast together. I tell myself an easy-like-Sunday-morning attitude would really be better for us all. Therein is the trap.

I dread Sunday mornings, but I'm always happy after we go to church. It's like spiritual exercise, and I know it's good and right to be challenged to learn, grow, and change. I want to be proactive and preempt the challenges life will inevitably bring. And I want to learn how to have a more positive impact on the world around me. That's what church is for.

On my own, I won't pursue that. I'm lazy. I'm a jerk. So, I need church. I need the spiritual exercise to grow. It's where I go to be built up in spiritual matters, leaving inspired to become a better person.

Diet, exercise, and church. It's a healthy combination.

#10 Christians

I was in a band called Strongarm. Psalm 89 in the Bible inspired the name. It talks about God delivering his people with his strong arm. Our name also had a double meaning as an indirect reference to Jesus. But mainly I picked it because it sounded tough.

Musically, we called ourselves hardcore. The style fell somewhere between metal and punk rock. Like punk, it was outspoken and raw. Like metal, it was heavy and a little more polished. Either way, if you heard Strongarm, you'd probably wonder what the heck we were saying and why we were so mad. The style was passionate, aggressive, and cleansing. I loved it. I still do.

I was the lead singer, but I can't really sing. So I was the screamer. I also wrote the lyrics. In fact, I wrote 15 of the 19 songs that are out there. But who's counting? And I ran most of our business affairs. By the time I quit, we'd recorded a full-length album, released a few singles on seven-inch vinyl records, shot a music video, and done several small tours. There's still a bunch of our merchandise floating around online auctions, if you're interested.

I learned a lot in the band. Overall, it was a great experience. Though I quit in 1996, I still get a few emails a month from avid fans. I'm always complimented and honored by their well wishes.

When our first album, *Atonement,* came out, we did something out of character. We did a tour of Christian venues. The opportunity came up, so we took it for the quick exposure to support the record. There were a lot of memories, like the last show of the tour when we stood around and shared how much we hated each other before going on stage. Did I mention we were all Christians?

We brought along a friend named Tom. He volunteered to be our roadie, helping us with extra muscle. This gave him an opportunity to travel the country for free. He didn't believe what we believed, but he was an amazing guy. We really liked him, and he liked our band. We also hoped the experience might have a positive influence on him. It influenced him all right.

One show in particular stands out. It was in Memphis. We arrived and were greeted by the promoter, who told us he'd received a call from our previous stop. They called to advise him that we weren't "Christian" enough. They recommended he cancel the show.

You see, our friend Tom had an underground magazine (called a zine). He hoped to promote it and make contacts on the tour. There was some slightly coarse language in it, but it wasn't a huge deal to us. It really wasn't any worse than what is on primetime television. We just asked him to hand it out on his own time and not from behind our merchandise table.

Anyway, a parent got hold of one of the zines and went ballistic.

So, we were horrified when we arrived in Memphis to accusations that our band promoted filth and pornography. At the time, we felt the parent's reaction was unwarranted. Tom felt terrible about jeopardizing our tour. We felt bad for him. But something even worse had happened.

This hit Tom hard. He just wasn't the same after that. He learned something about Christians. He learned to hate them. It's something I've always struggled with, because there always seems to be some type of fallout when they're around. The deeper issue was that Tom, like many, decided to stay away from Jesus. I don't know where Tom is today, but in the grand scheme of things, I wonder if it would have been better if he hadn't toured with us.

Nothing has discouraged me more in my desire to follow Jesus and know God than my observations of those who call themselves "Christians." They make it so easy to hate them. They can be crazy, annoying, judgmental, and hypocritical.

Even worse, I regret that each of those words also represents me personally, to some degree.

Crazy Train

Is it me, or does it seem like a lot of "Christians" are on a one-way commuter train to Crazy Town, listening to Looney Tunes while the train stops and picks up passengers from Strange Land and Bizarro World?

Our band's Memphis stop was legendary for other reasons. That's where we got a flat tire, were bombarded by an extraordinary number of money peddlers, and saw dozens of Godzilla-sized rats around town.

It's also where we met the "Apostle of a Different Gospel."

Our promoter, Matt, didn't cancel the show. After we unloaded our equipment, he took us to eat before the concert. This was always a good thing. On tour, everything's irregular. The lack of healthy food, plus inconsistent sleep, amplifies moodiness and causes the runs. Irregular was a way of life.

So far we really liked Matt and everything was going great, until he started talking. I mean *really* talking. What he shared started strange, became more judgmental, and finally harsh. We were polite and kept our comments brief. His words pinnacled as he proclaimed he intended to never sin again. "Jesus did it," he said, "so why can't I?"

We were dead silent. He sounded totally insane.

Unfortunately, the crazy kept coming.

We survived the meal and the awkward moments and were happy to get back to the venue. Once there, we set up our merchandise and finished our sound check. Matt asked if we wanted to pray before the show. We agreed and followed him to a back room. That's where we "prayed."

There was hollering, extended amounts of uncomfortable handholding and shoulder rubbing (we were all guys, mind you), and lots of weird sounds. It seemed to last forever and scared us a little. We were uncomfortable, but eventually it ended.

After the show, Matt put us up at his place. It was late and we were tired. We all went to our respective sleeping areas. As we started to settle in, we were awakened by a repetition of words.

For some reason, Matt—a grown man with no children—owned a Speak & Spell learning toy from the '80s. Through the course of the night, he was spelling strange things on it. He finally ended by going from room to room, spelling "systematic theology." To this day, I can see those crazy eyes peering affectionately over the toy in the dark as it repeated the letters in that hollow, expressionless computer voice, "S–Y–S–T–E–M–A–T–I–C–T–H–E–O–L–O–G–Y." It still haunts me.

All this earned him the name "The Apostle of a Different Gospel." We meant it to be humorous, but it really wasn't so funny. We knew we weren't perfect, but we also didn't want to be associated with that particular brand of those who claim to follow Jesus.

There was the woman I'd really looked up to who told me Jesus didn't like punk rock. She said he was okay with rock and roll, he even liked country a little, but preferred classical above all. It didn't take me long to realize that was also what she liked. I avoided her after a while, especially since I hate country music. I am still convinced it will be playing at sonic levels in hell.

Then there was the time I went to work at a warehouse while I was in college. My warehouse manager told me about a particular guy who worked in the office: "He's a Christian, so you probably want to stay away from him." One day I had to go into the office to ask the "Christian" about an order. The first thing I saw was an awkwardly huge Bible on the front corner of his desk. As time went on, I noticed it was always there. Everyone stayed away from him because his demeanor and habits were so strange. I didn't tell anyone there about my faith, because I didn't want to be associated with this "Christian."

Then there's the "Christian" merchandise—T-shirts that from far away look like they say "Enjoy Coke," but actually say "Enjoy

Jesus" upon closer inspection. Or the breath mints I saw called Testa-mints. Or fake twenty-dollar bills with a message from Jesus when you look closely. Don't they know normal people don't think that's cute?

I've never met anyone who's had a deep epiphany from a breath mint or a phrase on a T-shirt. Would anyone really respond with, "Boy, these mints really make your breath smell heavenly; tell me more about God!" Or, "I wanted a refreshing soda, but I think I'll let you tell me about Jesus instead. That sounds more refreshing!" Or, "I waited on you hand and foot and, instead of a tip, you left this piece of paper that looked like money, with a Bible verse on it. Thanks! I realized gas in my car didn't matter. What I really needed was spiritual riches!"

And let's not forget the "Christians" who say they're not allowed to dance or wear make-up, and men can't have long hair, and women can't have short hair or wear pants. These "Christians" do strange things that alienate others and make us all want to avoid them. They aren't exactly winning friends and influencing people.

I admit that after working in that warehouse, I bought a smaller Bible. It made me think. Actually, each Bible I've purchased has been smaller than the one before (like those Russian dolls that go from little to tiny). Today I have one that fits in my pocket. But I take it out when I get into church because I don't want anyone there to think I'm not "Christian" enough. Old habits die hard.

I think it's okay to be strange. Everyone has quirks and hang-ups. I'm just saying believing in God is strange enough. I don't want to make it worse. It's bad when my own quirks affect my representation of God and Jesus. That's when a personality quirk becomes a character flaw. More to the point, these tendencies can hurt people and leave a bitter taste for others about God.

How Soon Is Now?

As if being stocked-up on crazy isn't enough, Christians have more ways of making it worse. Sometimes they're so annoying with some of the things they do and say that you can't wait to get away.

Have you noticed that a lot of Christians talk in some type of code? It's as if they have another language. A conversation with them would go a lot better with one of those universal translators they use on Star Trek when talking to various life forms.

Christians use words that don't make sense. It's called Christianese. Here's a quick guide to help you with the most common terms in their code talking:

Blessed: Not a response to sneezing, but a term often describing something positive. It may be used in response to small-talk questions. Example: "How are you doing?" *"I'm so blessed!"* English synonyms: fine, great, good.

In the flesh (or worldly, lukewarm, not in-the-spirit): Describes a Christian who's not extremely religious or conservative and who's prone to make emotional, hasty decisions. He or she may even watch an R-rated movie or listen to music that's not "Christian." Synonyms: fair-weather fan, untrue, insincere, being human.

Brother: A term of endearment between male Christians. Women may use the female version "sister," but that's not as common. Synonyms: friend, pal, buddy, dude, bro, homey.

Pray about it: A phrase depicting a lack of confidence or comfort with a specific decision or situation. Synonyms: think it over, be careful.

Heathen (or non-Christian, nonbeliever, unbeliever): A term referring specifically to someone who doesn't believe in Jesus, or who may believe but hasn't decided to give Jesus his or her full devotion. Synonyms: not a Christian, not religious, doesn't believe in God/Jesus.

Backslider: Describes a person who is or was a Christian but who has relapsed into old, bad habits. Synonyms: being AWOL, playing hooky, MIA.

Fellowship: Describes socializing between Christians, something often viewed as critical to spiritual growth. Synonym: hanging out.

Convicted: Doesn't describe a criminal, but rather someone who's sensed a warning or something wrong in a particular area of his or her life or in regards to a specific choice or action. Synonyms: regretful, guilty, sorry, cautious.

Born again (or on fire, saved, have salvation): Describes a person who has come to a belief in Christianity or has experienced a spiritual rebirth through Jesus. Synonyms: having ownership, buy-in, enthusiasm.

Revival: This doesn't describe the shock paddles used in an ER when someone has flat lined. It does, however, share some similarities. Synonyms: a spiritual awakening or a renewed religious fervor.

Witness (or evangelize, give your testimony): A Christian shares with a non-Christian why he or she is, or became, a Christian. Synonyms: persuade, convince, influence.

Sometimes even when they don't use strange terminology,

Christians speak in ways that don't make sense. If you tell them you're being laid off at work, they might respond, "Everything happens for a reason." As if that's exactly what you needed to hear.

Or if your child is facing emergency surgery, a Christian might tell you, "All things work for good for those who love the Lord." Or if it's their own child, they might even say, "Praise the Lord!" or "I'm trusting God!" You feel like some Christians think they don't have problems like everyone else. It's annoying and alienating, because it's not always genuine.

And if that isn't enough, Christians want to talk about things that don't fit the conversation or that you don't want to talk about. Maybe you just want to go out for a cup of coffee and talk normal, about normal things, with normal responses. But you feel like they're just waiting for an opportunity to turn the conversation and try to "convert" you. Like, "Oh really? You mowed your lawn yesterday? That reminds me of something Jesus said about farming and about people who are going to hell." You think, *Just shut up or go away.*

Christians can come off as distant—like they don't live in the real world with the rest of humanity. You want to send them a post-card with a picture of earth and write on the back: *Wish you were here!*

It may sound weird, but I think Christians can be sincere without being authentic. Their intentions may be good, but they can come off as not very personal, real, or likeable, because they think if they don't seem perfect, they'll make God look bad. When, in fact, the exact opposite is true.

As they interact like this with people who aren't part of their particular social circle, culture, or subculture, it can alienate. It also inadvertently creates an insider/outsider, us versus them mentality.

I think the best and safest solution is to just talk normal. If Christians simply communicated in everyday language, they'd seem less freakish. But I could be wrong.

I actually don't talk Christianese. It might be the one flaw I don't have. Or maybe it's from not being spiritual—I'm just "in the flesh."

My Way

Christians can be judgmental too. Sometimes they love to tell others how to live, both directly and indirectly.

I once worked on a crew remodeling a house. There were about ten of us, and I was the new guy. At noon all the guys would get their lunches out of their trucks, sit down somewhere on the job site, and eat together, except for the Christian guy. He would go off and eat alone in his car. I asked the other guys about this. They said when he first started they invited him to join them, but he said he couldn't because they weren't "Christians."

Admittedly, it was difficult for me when these guys would pass around the latest issue of *Penthouse*. In one breath, they talked about their weekends, wives, and kids; in the next, they would comment on the centerfold's curves. I'd simply say, "No thanks," and casually stare down at my sandwich like I was thinking about something. I also avoided any conversation in the way of God or Jesus because of what the "Christian" did. I didn't want the other guys to think that's how God felt about them. They hated that "Christian." I tried to talk to him about it all, but he said I was too "worldly."

Christians do things like boycott Disney, hold up signs at funerals that say *God Hates Fags,* and bring fetuses to antiabortion protests. None of this does any good. People don't turn to God, or get any closer to him, from these misguided methods.

Many times they're the first to judge and the last to love. Why can't they get it through their thick skulls that Jesus never disliked those who didn't follow God or didn't know much about him? But he did get angry with people who claimed to follow God but misrepresented him.

They're judgmental toward each other too. "Christians" love judging other "Christians" and telling them how to live.

The band I mentioned almost never happened. The story of Strongarm's beginnings includes pain and anger.

When I was a teenager, I eventually found a church I liked. It was actually a Jewish temple. No, I'm not Jewish, but I had a friend in high school that was, and he believed in Jesus and so did the temple he went to. This wasn't typical, so I was curious when he invited a few friends and me to his "church." It was different—filled with joy and energy. I ended up really liking it, and some of us kept going.

It was like any other church, except there were all kinds of Jewish traditions and ceremonies incorporated into the service. This was awesome; because it really helped me better understand the Bible, which is saturated in Hebrew culture and history.

Rabbi Harvey (their equivalent to the lead pastor at a church) took a liking to my friends and me. Knowing we wanted to start a band, it wasn't long before he got behind us. He gave us the key and alarm code to the building so we could practice there. He said we could use the equipment and building anytime it wasn't being used.

We were surprised, since we were only teenagers, but we couldn't pass this up. It was much better than a garage.

Over the next year, we started writing songs and playing shows. It was going well. We were really growing as a band and as individuals. They were good times.

But one day Harvey asked to talk to us after the service. He brought us into his office and said he needed the keys back. *Was it something we did? Did we break something?* It was much worse.

He informed us that our music was opening a porthole directly to hell.

I admitted our music wasn't very good yet, but a doorway to hell seemed a little extreme. He half-smiled and told us the real story.

A woman in the church had a vivid dream that a doorway to hell had opened in her living room floor and pulled her children into it. She communicated that it was a result of our practicing our music in the church. She said it conjured up evil spirits because it was so heavy (which is another subject). She further explained that it was causing her children to rebel.

Harvey was sad about the situation. Of course, he didn't think there was anything to her story. But he explained that she was the wife of one of the other rabbis, their family was big, and they'd been there long enough that he had to take the easy road and diffuse the situation the simplest way.

We were devastated. From then on, we felt judged, like outcasts.

A few months later, we decided to find another church, one that was more welcoming. It was hard. In time, we eventually got over it and were able to put it into perspective.

Jesus was always a friend to those who didn't believe in God. Jesus even hated self-proclaimed "religious" people. It's what got him killed. He knew it would, but that didn't stop him. He wanted the entire world to know how much God, his father, loved them.

Sometimes Christians just need to get over themselves and loosen up.

Master of Puppets

Many Christians can also be quite hypocritical.

A few years ago when we were in Florida, my wife and I were sitting on the couch after dinner when we were startled by a huge crash that shook our whole house. I rushed out to find a crowd of kids and fathers around our garage door. One of the kids had driven a quad-runner straight into it and totaled the door. Fortunately, he wasn't hurt.

His mother showed up, yelled at him like crazy, and then reassured us they would take care of the costs to have our door repaired. "My husband is a pastor," she said. "We're Christians, and we do what we say. We fix our mistakes."

Later that night, she called me up, this time singing a different tune. She told me to call the builder (they were still building homes in the neighborhood) and tell them I didn't know how the damage happened. I was to say I'd come home to the problem and that it was probably the fault of some irresponsible subcontractor. She said they would probably take care of it for free.

I told her I wouldn't lie.

That's when she said I needed to call the quad-runner's owner and have him pay for it.

I said I wouldn't do that either.

Then she said her son wasn't supposed to be riding it. For that matter, she wasn't even convinced her son did it. And if that wasn't good enough for me, I would have to file a lawsuit. She wasn't paying a dime.

I never told her I was a Christian (and also a pastor at the time), but I reminded her that she was. I repeated her exact words and finished with, "If this is what it means to be a *Christian,* I don't ever want to be one."

That's when her talking got clumsy and quieter as she fumbled through a few responses. She clumsily hung up, and a few minutes later her husband showed up with a check delivered with many apologies. I noticed their check had one of those Christian fish symbols on it. And I guess they wrote it from a side-business, which was literally called Wise Decisions, Inc.

The irony.

Christians can be hard to put up with. I've had a few small businesses over the years, and all my worst customers have been Christians. In my current handyman business, I never tell anyone I'm a Christian. If they know I am (and they are too), without fail they try to squeeze some deal out of me or use it as leverage to receive special treatment.

I recently did a job for a woman I met at church. She wanted to replace her ugly gold dining room light with a newer one. She asked me to bring down my price. In her home, I noticed she had Internet, cable TV, a home phone, cell phone, and this new light fixture. But for some reason I was expected to help subsidize all that by bringing down my price for the light just because I'm a Christian. *If it's money you need, just ask.* That would be more sincere. I know I sound like a jerk, but Christians can be frustrating when they misuse their title.

I've also done my part. A couple years into Strongarm, I threw my weight around. I kicked a couple of the members out. Sure, I told them I thought it was what God wanted, that I'd prayed about it and all. They thought about it for while, but they couldn't argue, because I threatened to quit. It was them or me. Since I sang, wrote the lyrics, and ran most of the affairs of the band, I had all the leverage. And I knew it.

We were supposed to be friends. I should have just been honest. It was my own agenda and what I thought was best for the band. My approach was hypocritical, and I didn't handle it right.

If you ask me, a Christian should be the most generous and genuine of individuals. The best boss. The best employee. The best friend you could ever have. Unfortunately, that's not always the case. We can be fake.

So if you ever meet people who lead with "I'm a Christian"— just beware. They may be great people, but you never know. They might give you a reason to hate them.

All Apologies

I'm sorry.

Whether you are or aren't a Christian, I apologize on behalf of myself and all other Christians for all the things we do and have done over the years. I'm sorry we may have given you the wrong impression of what it means to be a follower of Jesus. I'm sorry we may have given you a wrong expectation of what it means to pursue this faith.

Let me be clear: we don't know everything, and we don't have all the answers.

There's no excuse for our bad behavior. Period.

At times we've lied, talked in ways you couldn't relate to, been insensitive, taken advantage of situations, and pretended to be holier-than-thou. We've been standoffish, not repaid loans, not paid for things we broke, harped on your mistakes while cheating on our own taxes, pretended to care, called you names behind your back, and been argumentative. We've thought we're always right, cut you off in traffic with our Christian stickers on the backs of our cars, been cheap, manipulated bosses, and talked to you in everyday conversations by using language you couldn't understand. For all that, and much more, please accept my sincerest apologies. We've alienated you, judged you, been condescending to you, been unreliable, sold you short, not helped, and not been there to encourage you when you needed it. We've taken the moral high ground while displaying a low quality of character at the same time.

It was and is all wrong.

I don't want to justify any of this. Just know that although we strive for perfection, as God encourages us to, we aren't perfect. We haven't arrived and we know it. Often we forget this or try to ignore it by bringing others down. In a twisted way, it makes us feel better, because deep down we know we're not the people we want to be or should be. Even though it's wrong, it makes it a little easier to face ourselves if we bring everyone else down a notch or two.

In our hearts, we really do hold something that we feel is priority one. It just gets scattered in the messiness of our own failings, stupidity, and pride.

Perhaps you might find a way to be patient with us in the same way you're probably patient with others who make no such claim.

Please be patient with us like you are with crazy football fans that paint themselves and put flags on their cars. They're annoying, but you don't necessarily hate them.

Or like you might be with the person with blue hair and a pierced lip. Or the one who wears those ugly T-shirts with wildlife on them. They look strange, but you probably don't hate them.

Or with the person who wears his pants too low. Or the preppie kid down the street. You don't get it, but you don't really hate them.

Please be patient with us like you might be with the accountant who talked to you about IRAs, 401Ks, S-Corps, C-Corps, and LLCs. You didn't really know what it meant at the time, didn't really care that much, but you weren't offended.

Or like I was while on tour with Strongarm. We stopped in Atlanta and visited the Underground. In the food court, I ordered a burger, and the cashier hollered to the back, "Put yo' foot in it!" I guess she saw the anxiety on my face as I imagined some medium-rare toe-jam. She calmed me with her southern-accented explanation: "Don't worry, honey. It just means be quick about it." What a relief.

You get the idea. We all hurt and confuse others from time to time, and we're all on the outside every once in a while. I know Christians make a lot of mistakes. We all do. The problem is, we should be the ones setting the example. When we claim a certain spirituality and devotion to God, but in reality misrepresent him, it really stands out.

Yes, every Christian is a hypocrite in some way and always will be. But please consider that when someone lives by a specific standard, or tries to, and everyone knows it, it's more noticeable whenever he fails, even a little.

I have a good friend who's a vice president at Coke. He's even more militant about Coke than I am. He won't eat in a restaurant that doesn't serve Coke products, not even on vacation. He justifies his quirk with this: "I better be loyal. Coke is sending my kids to college."

Once I caught him at a restaurant that didn't serve Coke, and I railed him. He seemed like such a hypocrite. But I forgave him.

Over the years, I've even had proud, self-proclaimed atheists and agnostics ask me, while going through a time of personal crisis, to pray for them. Though it was technically inauthentic and hypocritical of them to make such a request, I made no issue of it. Though in a sense it was a lapse in their integrity, I did it for them. Nobody's perfect.

Christians have crushed me too. Staying true when someone says you're opening up a porthole to hell isn't easy. As much as it broke my spirit to be treated like that, what I believed and knew to be true in my heart sustained me more than any amount of anger it kindled ever could. It was the harder route, but I knew it was right.

That's a real challenge.

So please be patient with us.

Maybe you could agree with me that even with our many flaws, some Christians deserve some credit. Historically, most hospitals, colleges, and world-relief efforts have been founded, funded, and sustained out of the generosity of followers of Jesus. They give like no one else does, sometimes financially, sometimes with their time, and sometimes with their very lives. There's something authentic about true followers of Jesus, though none are without flaws.

I don't want you to ever become a "Christian" in some of the negative ways I have described. You don't want to carry the guilt and regret from this like I do. I don't want you to join a religion. Don't ever be the freak, the funny talker, or the hurtful, judgmental person. Don't remove all reason and sense from a faith decision. It's frustrating and embarrassing. This doesn't free people at all. In contrast, it seems to limit and control. I wouldn't wish it on anyone.

It's a hard reality to admit that more people aren't open to the message of Jesus because of "Christians." If Jesus was and is real, then his followers need to represent him with the best evidence: changed lives.

Jesus said his followers would be known by their love. So maybe we should be committed to engaging others' curiosity through overwhelming displays of responsibility and compassion.

One day you might meet someone like that.

So please forgive us, and please be patient with us. And don't become a "Christian."

Losing My Religion

This last part is a word to Christians specifically.

When my wife and I hurt each other, it's always because one of us (usually me) is being inconsiderate, selfish, short, inattentive, distant, disinterested, self-centered, self-absorbed, etc. Since these traits often come naturally, when we sense the onset of such behavior, we casually say to the other, "Resist the urge to be your-self." We say it respectfully and with a hint of humor. We commit to not getting mad over it. It's a safe phrase we've created. And it works every time.

Here's my challenge to Christians: *Resist the urge to be yourself.*

It'll work every time.

And think about taking it to another level. Consider no longer calling yourself a "Christian."

Take a few seconds to think about what it would mean if you had to stop using that term to describe yourself. What would you have to do? Most likely, you'd be forced to do something drastic.

Above all else, you'd have to consider your attitude and actions in everything. Like never before, you'd have to take into account how you represent the truth hidden in your heart. At work. As a friend. As a neighbor. As a husband. As a father. As a mother. As a wife. As a son. As a daughter. As a boss. As a follower of Jesus. I think nothing would be more productive for you and the state of your faith.

I challenge you, for a season at least, to peel away the term "Christian" from your mind and remove it from your vocabulary. Do it for more than a week. Make it hard; do it for three months. That's a good test. Even mark it on your calendar as a reminder.

Furthermore, to make this part more interesting (assuming you've worked through the necessary adjustment to your attitude and actions), allow yourself to speak about your faith only when you're asked about it. (If no one's asking, you probably have more work to do on yourself.) And don't initiate conversations about God or the like. Your actions and attitude will have to be the catalysts. But when people do ask about how you handle anger, stress, hardships, failures, success, leadership, authority, and submission so well, you'll have a chance to talk. When they wonder why you're so forgiving and patient, why you won't compromise, why you remain respectful, why you always have time to talk, why you always have time to just listen—you'll have the opportunity to explain.

And since you can't use the term "Christian," you'll have to creatively explain what's going on in your life—and why. You'll have to find different ways to describe it. It may take some thought, but you can do it.

And if people happen to say, "Oh, you mean you're a Christian," that's fine. Don't make a scene. Just go with it. It's accurate. If they ask why you didn't just say that before, be honest. Tell them you're trying to redefine the term in your own life because of the bad reputation so many Christians have given Jesus and God.

This challenge will be difficult, but I believe it will work, and I'm willing to bet something revolutionary will happen.

If you really want to influence others in the name of Jesus these days, it will take desperate measures. You'll have to redefine yourself.

This challenge is exactly what made the early followers of Jesus so intriguing. Followers of Jesus were an underground movement that had no official title. They didn't have the benefit of a catchy one-word description that could easily lose it's meaning. They didn't call themselves "Christians."

In fact, that term wasn't even coined by the actual followers of Jesus. It was meant to be a joke, even a little jab.

People looked at these followers and were perplexed. Here was a strange bunch that did things differently than anyone else. They didn't avoid the diseased and crippled, as if God were punishing these individuals. They helped them. They didn't stay away from thieves, prostitutes, or any other "undesirable" types. They talked to them and even invited them over for dinner. They treated different ethnic groups, women, and children with equality. They even showed respect for corrupt leadership. They spent time with anyone and everyone.

As society observed these followers of Jesus, they saw a difference. They saw a loving and compassionate subculture, as if they were from another place, with another identity, and so the term *Christian* was born. If you were a follower of Christ, they called you that. Eventually, followers of Jesus embraced the term because it really was *Christ* who gave their lives meaning. They became proud to carry the title.

Before that term arose, they'd called themselves followers of "the way." I like that. Maybe it's something we can use again. It implies a lifestyle rather than a particular belief system. It's a call to action.

My hope is that followers of Jesus—followers of the way—will be known by their love, as Jesus said. I don't think others would hate these individuals. I wouldn't. Maybe then I could get over most of my issues with Christianity and stop rambling on.

Nothing would be more exciting than to see a new movement of apostles of the true gospel of Jesus. History is evidence of that. A movement of compassion, love, and responsible actions that inspires change would be unstoppable.

Or like I wrote about in the very last words in the very last song on the first and only Strongarm album I ever appeared on in a song called "Strengthened in Faith":

Though we become weary
It has been granted unto us
The ability to remain loyal
Unshaken in spirit

For those strengthened in faith
All things work for good
Hope for tomorrow
The perfecting of the saints

So, don't be a "Christian." Be something more. Become something better.

What Now?

When I was about eight, my father had a good friend who moved to Alaska to do deepwater salvaging. He wanted to satisfy his need to explore and try new adventures. I can't imagine scuba diving in Alaskan waters. I shiver just thinking about it. But it worked for him. Periodically, he would come back to South Florida to visit (probably to thaw out) and tell us about this strange way of life.

As he described it, Alaska sounded like the last place I wanted to be. He lived on a sailboat, which seemed a strange place to call home if you're in Alaska. That's a better fit for Florida.

I remember he said he once shot a bear with his revolver as it was trying to get in his boat. This also seemed odd to me, since everyone knows if you're living in the wild, you need a shotgun. A revolver will only make a giant, human-eating bear angry. It has no stopping power. You need something that can leave big gaping holes so you don't become a meat-popsicle for a beast like that.

He also explained that the hardest thing about living in Alaska wasn't the cold, the bears, or the long nights in the winter. The hardest thing, he said, was the loneliness.

Some handled it better than others. He told us about everyone in his town being awakened in the middle of the night by a man going around breaking all the windows. He was throwing things, shooting out storefronts, and breaking all the signs.

Soon the police showed up. They were natives, so they knew exactly what to do. They casually got out of their cars, and one officer slowly approached the offender while talking calmly. Eventually he reached the man and simply rested a hand on his shoulder. With this, the man's demeanor immediately changed. The rage and tension quickly diffused as the officer sympathetically communicated understanding and gave some much-needed human contact. The personal connection brought him back.

All the man needed was a touch to get back some perspective and soothe his restless soul. He was lost. He'd forgotten who he was and what he was doing. He'd lost focus and let his emotions take over. The warmth and compassion changed his outlook right away. It was as if blinders lifted from his eyes, and he was able to see the world in his right mind again.

My father's friend said this kind of thing is common at the end of longer winters. That's when people snap. Sometimes the tension builds up and engulfs them, and they do things they know are wrong and destructive, but they just can't stop. Their passion takes them to places they can't control—places of tension and frustration that build into pure, unbridled aggression.

Sometimes I deal with the same kind of internal aggression. I don't like it, but I seem to balance on that emotional edge a lot. There are times when we all get stir-crazy down to the deepest levels of our souls. That's when life gets dark.

I've discovered frustration, tension, and sometimes anger in regard to the most important part of my life—my faith. So I've tried to hate for a reason, and be somewhat productive with it, because I'm convinced I'm not the only one.

Knowing that somebody understands, and has gone through the same thing, can be saving knowledge. This has gotten me through tough times. Candid conversations with friends have brought much needed relief. That's what I hope this book can be for you in matters of faith.

When I thought of the idea for this book, I shared it with several people. Some were total strangers; some were close friends. The responses were clear and decisive each time. They fell on two sides and never in-between.

Some gave resounding approval and support: "I totally relate." "I've felt the same way and just never said it like that." "People need to hear that."

From others, I got blank stares or half-smiles. "Do you have to say *hate?* How about *really dislike?*" It was hard not to laugh. I could never take seriously a book entitled *10 Things I Really, Really Don't Like About Christianity.*

I had to say *hate* because it best represents the challenges that hit me and how I feel when they do. And I had to believe there were people out there like me—people drawn to bare-bones honesty, who get tired of pretense and hidden agendas.

I just wanted to share out in the open the things we all think behind closed doors. In a strange way, this book is meant to be an encouragement; because I have a feeling we all reach certain impasses in our lives we need help getting around.

I'm convinced that many, many people are moved by the teachings and person of Jesus. They want to believe. They want to follow. They just get disconnected on some level, and somewhere along the way, they can't work through it.

That's why I had to write *this* book. So we can be firm in our beliefs. So we can follow more closely.

Most of the time, true difficulty—the kind that has the ability to create personal upheaval—is something that just has to be endured. In such a time, I believe there's a bit of relief knowing that someone else understands and identifies with the feeling. I hope somewhere in these pages you've found something to connect with, something to help you reconnect with God.

The most dangerous thing to do in such times is to stay isolated and not talk about what's going on. This book is filled with my angst-ridden frustrations. And talking about what's going on is the only thing that keeps me from falling over that edge of bitter anger. This open communication keeps me from falling over that fateful edge and dying inside.

I know I'm pretty screwed up. I can be pretty manic and moody. I struggle with small bouts of depression. I live on that thin line between love and hate way too much. I'm not bragging. I'm not proud. But I'm working on changing. That's really the point of it all, isn't it?

I've come a long way through my faith and working on how I understand my faith. Sometimes we all need a little help finding a way through the confusing terrain that is life. Sometimes we need help developing the right expectations. That's really the most important thing you can do in life.

This book isn't really about answers and facts. Sometimes they don't help all that much. Just try putting together a piece of furniture from IKEA; it comes with directions, but you're bound to mess it up unless you talk to someone who's actually done it. Answers alone don't always help, but combined with the right expectations, your experience can be dramatically different. The right expectations will help you decipher, navigate, and succeed in life.

I know I talked a lot about marriage and family in this book. That's because those are the most important arenas of my life. That's where my expectations have often destroyed me. It's where I've had to learn the most lessons, since that's where my maturity and perspective have been stretched the most. Because that's where I have to actually apply my faith—where it's tested.

Marriage has been hard. My wife and I have been married since 1999, and it has been frustrating for us. We grew up in divorced homes, and most of our friends came from divorced homes, a common trend for our generation. As a result, we've never seen or been around a healthy married couple on a consistent basis. Sometimes, with the more difficult things in life, you just have to see an answer acted out in order to learn. Just reading about it and talking about it has so many limitations. You have to see how it works. Well, we'd never seen how marriage works, not a good marriage that we wanted to imitate at least.

To say we've become frustrated with marriage is an understatement: arguments, fights, cussing, throwing fists, and holding grudges. But we know one thing for sure: we want to stay together. You see, we've had to learn everything, and I mean *everything,* about marriage through our own experiences, the good and the bad. Now that's normal to a degree—to figure things out for yourself (the hard way)—but not in everything.

We never had mentoring and coaching—out of old wisdom and tested character—about what to expect in marriage, and how to develop the right expectations. Which is why, whenever a conversation lends itself, we share all we can with other couples.

We tell them that even when a marriage is meant to be, it's still hard. And we assure them that since they said, "I do," it's meant to be. We tell them, "You won't always get along." We let them know they're even going to feel like leaving sometimes. We tell them to talk openly all along the way, no matter the pain. We tell them to sit down and communicate what's going on in their hearts; otherwise, they'll surely become distant and kill their intimacy. We tell them this is all part of the process of becoming one, since staying one is the real battle. We tell them that the relationship is naturally set to fail, that they have to actively pursue success in order for it to work.

We tell them what to expect so they can work through their frustrations a little bit easier, equipped with the knowledge that it's normal. We want to help them develop the right expectations so they can find their way, so they can make it *together.*

That's my goal in every area of life: to develop the right expectations in marriage, the right expectations in parenting, the right expectations about work, the right expectations with friendships. And to develop the right expectations in my faith—my first priority.

So talk it out with God too. I don't think he's offended by our raw, bold conversations. Even Jesus reached this point with God. In the garden of Gethsemane, he spoke openly and directly to his Father. He knew what was coming (his death), and he didn't like it. It was as if he said to God, "I don't want to do this. I hate the idea of it. But I'll do what I need to."

This book is me sitting on the counseling couch having it out with God. Telling him how I feel and trying to find my way. Staying committed to the relationship and trying to work it out. Trying to stay on the side of love and not hate.

Maybe you can work on the things you hate and bring them to the conversation.

× × × ×

I have to finish by asking, *Where are you in all this?*

I grew up in Florida, so Disney is in my blood. The first movie I ever cried over was *The Fox and the Hound*. Though I saw it while we were on vacation in Sweden, and it was dubbed in Swedish, the story still impacted me as a child.

One of the greatest things about having kids is watching that magic become part of their imaginations. It's like I get to relive the childhood memories and fun all over again when we watch movies and visit the parks together as a family. When Disney does kids' stuff, it's unmatched and always imitated.

My middle son loves *Toy Story 2*. He always chooses it when it's his turn to choose at movie time. There's something about *Toy Story 2* that gets me too.

One scene actually chokes me up. The main character, Woody, thought that life was all about playing and having fun. Sure, that's part of it, but he discovers that's just not all there is. He discovers there's more. He finds out the context of it all.

At the beginning, Woody is forgotten, lost, stolen, and kidnapped. He wakes up in foreign surroundings with strange toys. He's disoriented and scared. The other toys approach him, and he steps back confused. They know who he is; they know his name; they know what's going on and are thrilled to see him. The more they talk, the more terrified he gets. The tension and fear build.

One of the other toys sees his apprehension and reaches out to him. Everything's suddenly suspended and quiet, as the other toy reassures Woody: "Why... you don't even know who you *are,* do you?"

He really didn't. Woody never knew why he had a hat. He never knew why he had a badge and a gun. He never knew why his string, when pulled, said phrases like, "Reach for the sky, Buckaroo!" He didn't realize it all meant something.

He discovers that he's a sheriff. He figures out he's a good guy. He learns he's the one who saves the day. He comes to understand that he's part of a bigger story. Woody finds meaning as he finds his purpose in the bigger picture. Sure, he's a toy, but it's really about all of us.

You're part of a bigger story.

There's a reason for your personality, gifts, abilities, temperament, and experiences. There's context for why you are who you are. I want you to be fully committed with all of who you are, with your whole being, to figuring this out. Do whatever you have to do to make it all come together.

Since I was fifteen, I've been trying to follow the teachings of Jesus and to seek God's purpose for my life. That's the context that fit for me. It was the way. I believe it's the context for all of us.

My awakening was catalyzed by a conversation about life, family (oddly enough), meaning, and the future. This wasn't an uncommon curiosity for me. I'd lain awake many nights thinking on such questions. But that night I heard something for the first time. Or at least it registered differently this time.

I learned I had purpose and value. There was meaning to my existence.

It was different than the anecdotal pep talks from teachers. I was simply told, "You were created for a reason. There's a purpose for your life. You're important." When these words were spoken, they entered my ears and seemed to fill my heart. It was like I was instantly given a new perspective.

It was real, and it was deep. It was the truth I'd been missing and seeking without even realizing it. It was as if something was healed inside, something broken was restored, something lost was found. I was put back to the way I was meant to be, what I was originally created for. It was just right, and I can remember it like it was yesterday. My consciousness and sense of awareness were elevated in that moment, and I started anew.

This new beginning is what you've read about. While striving for perfection and change, I haven't been perfect. That's the point. I have, to the best of my ability, at this juncture in my life, tried to share my experiences. I've shared ten essential and foundational aspects of my faith; I hope they can help as you search for your context.

And know this: as difficult, confusing, and frustrating as my faith decision has been, it's the best decision I've ever made.

Perhaps you believe in God from a distance. Sometimes I do. Since my initial decision, I've often felt far from him and his touch. The hard times in life and difficult decisions have brought long, lonely spiritual lulls. Contrary to what many think, being a follower of Jesus is easier said than done.

There's an abundance of cynicism, pessimism, and negativity out there. And I'm no exception. I've known a lot of confusion, anger, and frustration since I was young. I suppose many of the feelings were the result of family stuff, but I also know they're common to this broken human experience.

It may defy logic and undermine intellectualism, but my faith has also brought clarity, peace, and comfort like nothing else. It has been the hope to inspire me on.

Everyone's on a journey that brings him or her either closer to God or further away. I believe that if you seek God with all sincerity and honesty, you'll find him.

And he'll find you. Beyond logic. Beyond the discomfort. Beyond the mystery of exclusivity. Beyond theology. God will meet you.

Consider rewriting your story. It will take courage, but there's a new beginning waiting for you.

Acknowledgments

Although the following people may not want to admit that they know me (given the title and content of my book), I would like to acknowledge their value and the impact they have had in my life. And if you wanted to remain anonymous, I apologize for mentioning you.

I would like to thank my wife, Lisa. I would never have been able to write this book without her love, support, and inspiration. And without her, my life would be meaningless. In many ways, she is the perfect wife and ideal mother. She is honest, principled, and working to be better. To me, that is perfection.

I would like to thank my kids, Aiden, Logan, and Carson. They are too young to care about or understand this, but one day they will. So I want to share how much they mean to me. Each one is unique in his personality and gifting and has taught me something about life, God, and myself. Thank you, my sons.

Thank you to Mat John. He has been a friend and brother since high school. Although being openly Christian in high school didn't make us particularly popular, it was a formative experience in my life. I have always valued his direct approach with me. I wouldn't be the person I am today without his friendship. And him and his wife have been my examples of love through sacrifice and compassion.

Thanks to Bob Franquiz for being one of my best friends. When we met, we became instant friends, like kindred spirits. We loved food, Coke, sci-fi, rock music, and the life of Jesus. What else is there? I kicked some members of Strongarm out to make room for him. I wanted him to share in the mission of the band. And sharing his mission of starting Calvary Fellowship in Miami Lakes, Florida, is one of the most important things I have ever done. I will always be grateful that he was crazy enough to make me an ordained minister. It stretched me in ways I needed.

And thanks to Bill LaMorey. He has been one of my best and most necessary friends. Without a doubt, he is the funniest person I have ever known. And I mean that as a compliment. His storytelling skills, mixed with his humor, have inspired me as I tried to capture my own personality in much of the narrative in this book. I will always admire him for starting Calvary Fellowship in West Hartford, Connecticut, from scratch. He always finds a way—between me laughing at him—to encourage me.

Thanks to Dave Katz for helping me decide on the missing chapter when I reached an impasse in the planning process of this book. While it seems so obvious to have a chapter on love in a book like this, I just didn't get it.

Thank you to Thomas Womack for cleaning up my manuscript and speaking words to me that helped me bring it to completion.

Thank you to Loyal Thurman and crew. They helped bring some inner healing I didn't even realize I needed and reignited a passion that had been dormant since I quit Strongarm so many years ago.

And thank you to all the Strongarm fans that have continually emailed me over the years. The fan sites and friend networks have always been encouraging. To hear the ways in which the lyrics I wrote so many years ago impacted your lives, or even saved your lives, is truly humbling.

And thank you to those not mentioned. Know that I have found value in every relationship over the years and have learned something from every friend I have. Who knows? Maybe you're better off being anonymous.

And, of course, thank you God—my Lord, father, savior, and friend. Although that is all very confusing, it doesn't make it any less true. Thanks for being patient with my mild insanity. In the end, my purpose for this book is to bring honor to you.

Acknowledgments

About the Writer

I grew up in Fort Lauderdale, Florida, and started my first band at the age of sixteen. It was horrible. By age twenty, my third band, Strongarm, was better. We signed with Tooth & Nail Records. We recorded an album, shot a video, went on several small tours, and also recorded a single as we prepared a second album. Halfway to completing it, I decided to quit the band, which ended my musical aspirations. The other members continued without me for a couple of years.

After leaving the band, I started a small construction company and finished school. After eight short years, I finally finished with an associate's degree in mass communications and a bachelor's degree in theology. In 2000, I helped start a church in Miami called Calvary Fellowship. I served as an assistant pastor overseeing several areas of ministry, including children and youth programs, volunteer placement, and lay counseling. At the end of 2005, I decided to make a change and follow another ambitious childhood dream—writing. *10 Things I Hate About Christianity* is my first project and, if all goes well, will be the first of many. Meanwhile, I operate a handyman business to pay the bills.

My wife and I have been married since 1999. We have three sons and attend North Point Community Church in Alpharetta, Georgia. We lead a small group there and volunteer in various ministry areas from time to time.

My blog is MorethingsIhate.com and I am available for speaking, freelance writing, and personal coaching. Please visit my site for scheduling and to watch for future projects.

Notes

1. "I tell you the truth, everyone who lives in sin is a slave to sin"—John 8:34 (NCV).

2. weeding out "everything that causes sin and all who do evil"—Matthew 13:41 (NIV).

3. think on things that are pure, good, holy, and respectable—Philippians 4:8.

4. King David danced—2 Samuel 6:14.

5. negative consequences to certain actions—Galatians 6:7.

6. to behave decently and not get drunk—Romans 13:13; Ephesians 5:18.

7. people who get drunk often become poor—Proverbs 23:21.

8. Jesus reinforced this rule—Mark 7:21, for example.

9. He took it to a higher level—Matthew 5:27-28.

10. not to get tattoos—Leviticus 19:28.

11. a gift to God to help build their temple—Exodus 35:22.

12. beautiful ornaments that God himself provided—Ezekiel 16:11-12.

13. avoid corrupting or unwholesome talk, and only speak appropriate words that have a positive, helpful impact—Ephesians 4:29.

14. dirty, foolish talk and crude jokes are out of bounds—Ephesians 5:4.

15. bless God in one breath, then curse someone in the next—James 3:9-10.

16. Jesus came to give us a rich and exciting life—John 10:10.

17. the story of the Good Samaritan—Luke 10:25-37.

18. "Love one another the way I loved you"—John 15:12 (The Message).

19. The Golden Rule—Matthew 7:12.

20. "Love your enemies. Do good to those who hate you..."—Luke 6:27-28 (NCV).

21. Two times when Jesus got violent with people—John 2:13-17; Luke 19:45-48.

22. "I gain nothing if I do not have love..."—1 Corinthians 13:3-8 (NCV).

23. hell in the Old Testament—Deuteronomy 32:22; Numbers 16:30; Job 7:9; 10:21; 11:8; 24:19; Psalms 18:4-5; 116:3.

24. Jesus also talked a lot about hell—Matthew 8:12; 10:28; 18:9; 23:33; Mark 9:44; Luke 16:23; Revelation 21:8.

25. just one cool drop of water on his tongue—Luke 16:19-31.

26. hell originally created for the devil and his demons—Matthew 25:41

27. "the book of life"; "a lake of fire"—Revelation 20:11-15.

28. A new age will start with a new way of living—Revelation 21–22.

29. extraordinary picture of heaven—Revelation 21–22.

30. the "book of life"—Revelation 21:27.

31. "For God so loved the world..."—John 3:16-17 (NIV).

32. all the general brokenness will one day be fixed and healed—Acts 3:21.

33. dinosaurs in the Bible—Psalm 74:13; Job 40:15; 41:1.

34. demise of the dinosaurs—see The Genesis Record by Henry M. Morris (Grand Rapids, Michigan: Baker Book House, 1976).

35. See Noah's Ark: A Feasibility Study by John Woodmorappe (Institute for Creation Research Publ., 1996).

36. dimensions of the ark—Genesis 6:14-21.

37. "Everyone has sinned and fallen short of God's glorious standard"—Romans 3:22-24 (NCV).

38. all of which are sins—1 Corinthians 6:8-10.

39. "I am the way, and the truth, and the life. The only way to the Father is through me"—John 14:6 (NCV).

40. "I tell you the truth, whoever hears my word and believes him who sent me..."—John 5:24 (NIV).

41. "I am the resurrection and the life..."—John 11:25-26 (NIV).